I cannot explain the mystery, the magic, the forces that have created you.
I can tell you, though, that you deserve to completely forgive and love your Self.
And that once you do, you will know the unknown.

AKAL PRITAM

self love

FINDING PEACE AND HAPPINESS

ROCKPOOL
PUBLISHING

contents

I am
a virgin.

Each moment is new.
Never been before.
Each kiss never before felt.
Each touch a new sensation.
Penetration into virgin lands.
New energies exchanged.
Only love remains as
another petal opens.
Beauty continues to unfold.

you have to be with
yourself more than
any other♡
it's way more enjoyable
if you love yourself
madly, deeply,
truly~
xx
o

the age of aquarius

As we enter the Age of Aquarius, there is potential for an evolutionary renaissance of humanity led by the heart.

The Age of Aquarius is the Energy Age, ruled by awareness, information and a new, expansive energy that will open our hearts. This age is all about individual empowerment and acting from conscious thought to create collective change.

As the world around us reflects our inner world, our founding relationship is to Self and soul. Without a loving relationship with ourselves we cannot serve others or heal the planet. Humanity, as it exists now, is severed from its roots, its spiritual bloodline, and the majority of us feel cut off from experiencing what should be an inherent prosperity and true happiness. At the core of our being, the energy of our soul, our true Self, exists along with all the beautiful human principles of self-love, kindness, sincerity, noble leadership and service to all others. When we can trust and use this inherent human power in a loving way, we can realise our full potential.

In the Aquarian Age, we are encouraged to learn through our own experiences and our own 'moral' compass, rather than follow what an 'authority' figure might tell us. Being a constant student, experimenting with and experiencing new depths of your own life is empowering.

A willingness to learn from mistakes, forgive all, maintain an open heart and a meditative mind leads to joy, the most powerful energy to heal and create positive change.

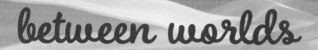

between worlds

In the Universe, there is no such thing as a secret.

If you are ready to enquire and listen, knowledge is revealed to you. As the Universe exists within you, the way to know the Universe is to know yourself. As the East continues to meet the West, ancient sciences that offer insights and meditative practices that heal are shared and learnt. Subtle individual and planetary energies and the changes that occur during solstices; eclipses and other significant astrological events are being honoured as we grow wiser.

In this Aquarian Age, our planet travels 'between worlds', also known as the Pleiades Photon Belt – a higher frequency of energy, and a purification and cleansing zone. This energy of pure consciousness alters the electromagnetic field of Earth. As our own electromagnetic field is intertwined with the Earth's, we are also affected. In this age, light information, including the blueprints of our DNA, which afford quantum leaps in evolution, stream through our planet. Information travels through light (think optic-fibre cable). Light carries the codes for life and evolution.

As we learn to tap into the power of the infinite, subtle energy of the Universe, we can heal from the past.

With mature, heart-centred action we can learn to appropriately harness the abundant energy of the Universe to create a prosperous and peaceful future.

the
truth
is,
you are
every thing.

the energy of change

The choice to exist with our own inner peace creates stability through all changes.

We can learn and practise authentic self-love so we can drop all our aggression, first to Self and then toward all else.

The creation of our species drew upon energy from the animal kingdom, yet it has always been our evolutionary opportunity to rise above basic animalistic characteristics. As our species matures, we activate and express the subtle and refined nature of our long heritage. The zodiacs inform us of our positive and negative animalistic traits. For example, the Lion is within us all and we are familiar with its primitive and refined characteristics. The challenge of this Universe's polarity game is to make mature choices about how we translate animal energy. Like the Lion, can we use our inherent powers to communicate our individuality in a noble manner, both self-protecting and respectful of others? Are we willing and able to master our own energy to enable us to share resources, relate and integrate with each other?

Each generation is bringing more Universal wisdom than the previous, and so, this way, we must protect and listen to our children and observe their perceptions and solutions. Like canaries in a coal mine, children inform us where toxic energy exists. Children also have a great deal of innovative and imaginative creativity to offer.

the centre of your existence

This is ancient knowledge that is rarely spoken about, yet it is vital to lasting transformation and, once understood, will change your whole life.

The centre of your existence is rooted behind the navel point, which is approximately three fingers below the belly button.

To be an empowered individual, you need to know how to tap into your infinity, harness it, circulate it and raise it with awareness (kundalini energy) up through the heart. Studying and practising some form of authentic yoga such as Kundalini yoga will give you an experience and tangible physical understanding of this.

To be vibrant and prosperous, you should engage your navel point in every aspect of your life. It is the first and most important point in a human body and it develops before the heart and brain. From this root of the soul, energy branches outwards through the body. If our education is only toward the brain, then our connection to our true power is never acknowledged and we can feel powerless. The accumulation of knowledge means nothing without the awareness that comes from a deep connection to the energy of the soul. If these branches of life that come from the soul are weakened through a closed heart, true love for ourselves or others can never really blossom. To be centred, we should flow outwards like a star from this point.

The brain takes time to respond to life, yet the navel point always responds immediately. Awareness from our soul halts over-thinking and moves focus to the 'wiser' frontal lobe of the brain.

the world is
your reflection
love
everything
be love
let your
love
flow

You were born as

liquid love.

wild.

I am free.

I am love.

I am miraculous.

finding true north

Your true north can be better understood by the position of the North Node of the Moon in your natal birth chart.

The North Node of the Moon is often called your soul purpose or dharma. Your dharma is based around service to others and will bring great happiness.

Self-love and the energy of the Heart Chakra is central to lighting your dharmic path. When you live from the awakened heart and the higher centres of your psyche, you become radiant and attractive.

A radiant individual can see where they are going more clearly, just like driving a car with headlights on at night remarkably improves your vision and protects you from crashing.

When you work to move pranic energy through your body, you create a more radiant body. In particular, yogic practices that use the breath along with movement and sound, such as Kundalini yoga and meditation, are highly effective. When you move pranic energy through the seven centres of psyche – the Chakras – you bring awareness up from the lower Chakras into the heart and the higher centres. The lower Chakras below the diaphragm are 'me' centric and don't bring happiness. When you bring the life force up into the open heart, you are able to act from a 'we' perspective. With life force in the higher centres of intuition and wisdom, your dharma is clear and the mind becomes interested in service and life beyond the material world. When you self-love, you are willing to open yourself up to finding your true North and happiness, which is of benefit to everyone.

what is love?

Love is a powerful, subtle energy that doesn't change with any condition; rather, it opens up space for all creation.

Love exists in everything that has been birthed for soul purpose. As this frequency has no resistance to expansion, it attracts life itself. Love dissolves fear and draws out the best qualities of existence and creative expression. Fear can only temporarily hold back self-expression because the Universe supports expansion and draws life from any dark space. Love facilitates the process of enquiry via a protective energy surrounding learning and continuous change. Love is flexible, it accepts mistakes and holds space for discovering the unknown.

Where there is love, there is a capacity for us to exist together with enough space for self-expression and improvement. Love is directed with a meditative mind, and although you can't see this subtle energy you can feel the effects. Love creates more space within you to be your true Self, to be open to change, to forgive yourself and others, to feel compassion, to integrate light and dark and receive life. If we believe stories, like 'things never change', 'we are separate from others', 'we are unworthy', or 'our true Self will not be accepted', we know our ego is speaking.

The frequency of love is close to the energy of liberation and freedom and should not be confused with blind fascination, desire, attachment or co-dependency. Love has nothing to do with a bind to another; instead, true love's expansive energy lets things go their own way. If we love someone dearly, we are willing and able to let them follow their own life path, wherever that may take them. With love we trust in the infinite, creative energy of our soul, our purpose, our ability to serve others and our deservedness to be happy.

... and the heavens opened ...

"I AM EAGER

"AND LOVE WILL REIGN AND THE GIANT EARTH WILL HEAL..."

YAY! every cell in her body cheered. (think endless mexican wave

she said

I LOVE YOU XOX DARLING

"I am going

How many drops in an ocean?

I love you

First.

oh darling heart

I love you so much

and then she

and it rained for days and everything was washed and when the clouds parted everything was joy.

green, the colour of healing, the colour of the heart chakra, cleansing, vibrancy, life...

laughed and

I love you

I love, love, love you

laughed and

You are so very beautiful

jumped with JOY

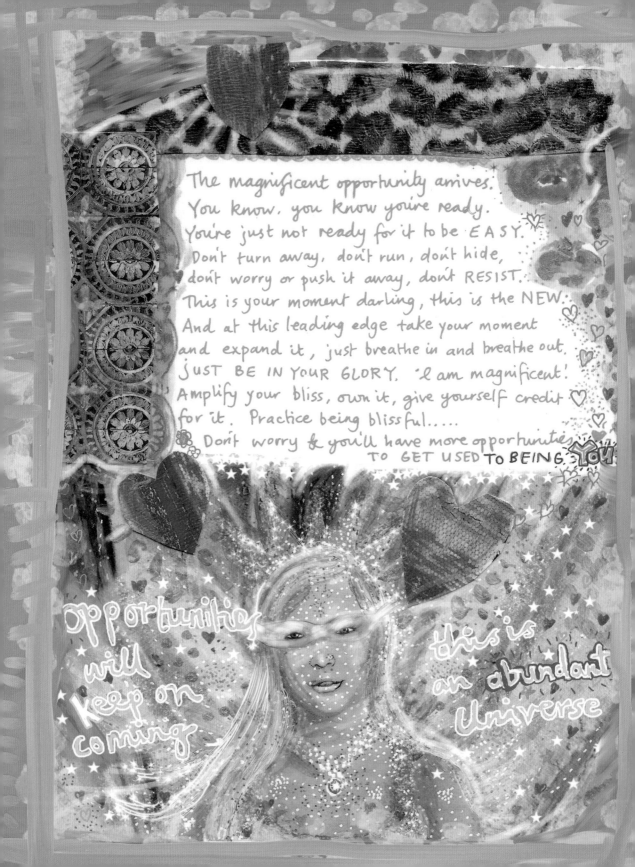

The magnificent opportunity arrives.
You know, you know you're ready.
You're just not ready for it to be EASY.
Don't turn away, don't run, don't hide,
don't worry or push it away, don't RESIST.
This is your moment darling, this is the NEW.
And at this leading edge take your moment
and expand it, just breathe in and breathe out.
JUST BE IN YOUR GLORY. 'I am magnificent'.
Amplify your bliss, own it, give yourself credit
for it. Practice being blissful.....
Don't worry & you'll have more opportunities
TO GET USED TO BEING YOU

opportunities will keep on coming

this is an abundant Universe

cultivating self-love

As tempting as it is to separate yourself from all else and indulge in self-judgement, blame and belittling criticism, know the frequency at which you vibrate affects everything.

When you take responsibility to heal your Self and practise a self-loving attitude, your positivity liberates others. Cultivating love for oneself means adopting positive, habitual ways of thinking about yourself. The most efficient way to do this is to forgive yourself and others and release the source of your patterns of thinking that led you to live as if you are limited and inadequate. When you focus your attention on negative energy, even an attempt to be rid of it, you give it energy. First, cultivate a kind and loving way to view your past and yourself and practise this vigilantly. It's also vital to release the inherited, negative imprints on your psyche.

One approach to healing is to practise authentic yoga. Ancient yogic science and technology offers healing medicine for deeply rooted patterns and empowers individuals to self-heal. Yogic teachings that offer mudra and mantra with movement work, because they connect the areas of the body and brain that need healing and re-integrating with the rest of the body and mind. These practices also focus on creating a straight and flexible spine, which is vital for feeling good about yourself and life itself. With consistent practice, fears around lack and imperfection dissolve; instead, a fertile soil is created for you to cultivate self-love.

ho'oponopono
a forgiveness practice

I am sorry. Please forgive me. I love you. Thank you.

Most of us are not taught to self-appreciate or self-forgive at a level that totally honours the true Self.

The Ho'oponopono is a simple practice of forgiveness from the ancient Hawaiians and is helpful to work through any layers of the psyche that no longer serve you. The key is to be patient and consistent. The Ho'oponopono practice is very valuable for situations where you feel emotional pain. This may be a partnership, a family relationship or a larger issue that causes you stress – environmental, animal or human rights. You practise this forgiveness within yourself. When you can see the whole picture in any situation, and understand your ability to serve others, you will find happiness. Remember you are a creator; you get to 'vote' for the kind of world you want to live in, with your intentional thoughts. When you learn to un-love yourself, you lose connection to the fundamental relationship with your soul. When you are disconnected from your soul and source you feel incomplete, flawed, bad, wrong, or ineffective. Yet you are missing nothing – you are complete within yourself and whatever you ask for is given. Healing and happiness come quickly when you forgive yourself completely and limitlessly.

The idea that anyone or anything is wrong is a result of self-deception from the mind. Life is not for tolerating; it is for learning, loving and excelling. Tolerance is a very heavy vibration and, ultimately, if you live by tolerating yourself, others and your experiences, you will deflate. When you feel deflated you send a signal to the ego to inflate you. Instead of suffering, find the enjoyment of serving others and acknowledging that everything in life is your teacher.

Your life is actually just one very beautiful opportunity to ultimately live in joy.

change begins with gratitude
I AM GRATEFUL for all that is, for my source of my existence and...
I AM INFINITE
I AM GRATEFUL I chose to come here in this body.
I AM GRATEFUL for this moment, for this opportunity, for my open heart
I AM CONNECTED
focus on what is real what is true, expand
You have abundance.
I AM GRATEFUL for my breath, my heart beat my body and...
I AM GRATEFUL for eyes to see, a mouth to speak, hands to touch and...

Kiss it
Kiss it
better
baby.

Ho'oponopono

I understand
myself
more
and
more,
that's all
I need, self
clarity,
then everything
is all glittery
& bright.

Some have
said I am
just all
'butterflies
& flowers'
good I
say!
They're
pretty,
gentle,
kind,
cute,
lovely,
& bring
I LOVE me
you to joy!

"The meek shall
inherit the earth."
True.

I am strong
enough to
forgive.

ho'oponopono

I am sorry

I allowed myself to experience pain through an emotional body perspective. I understand that I am not a victim and so I take a deep breath into my navel point and reignite my power. As I still my mind and unpack the contents of this situation, I can see more clearly. My life is my reflection and I acknowledge I am connected to everything.

please forgive me

I understand that self-forgiveness of how and why I allowed this situation to cause me pain and block my capacity to serve others is of utmost importance. Sometimes I mistake a situation and feel as though I am powerless. I now refocus my energy on being of service. I am present and aware as I take a deep breath into my heart and feel my universality. I let go of negative thinking and ego-based fears. I have the power to choose how to protect and project myself in this and all moments. I bless others and leave them to live their own life and I bless myself with deep appreciation for continuously practising to be love.

I love you

I love myself, and how I think and talk about myself always reflects this. I understand that my negative mind will perceive situations in a specific way in order to protect me, but with wisdom I do not make these perceptions my truth. My truth is that I am beautiful, bountiful and blissful. I accept and appreciate myself and this situation, which I see as a divine lesson.

As I open my heart more, I find the courage to face this situation.

thank you

I wish no one harm. Holding on to anger and resentment is poisonous. I thank myself for releasing all disharmonious energy. Without any regrets, I thank myself, others and this situation for teaching me.

I appreciate this opportunity to be of service, more aware and able to access my personal grit to rise above testing situations. I trust myself to learn from this situation.

I access my inner wisdom to free myself and others from the chains of the past. I am thankful for the power of my heart and my soul's guidance.

go on...

Ho'oponopono practice should ultimately be a celebration of release and empowerment that should lead to happiness.

Play the Ho'oponopono song to bring some Hawaiian lightness into the close of this practice (see resources). Also dancing the hula as you sing will elevate your energy, opening your hips, power centre, heart and throat and will keep your spirits high. There is something else to consider with this practice: if you set your heart on something, your head will give in. The mind must serve the heart. Be aware that the heart can have bitter passion. Be kind, to ensure you are acting purely withs self-compassion and an open heart. You know purity of intention when you have activated your intuition, your Third Eye. Passion is what drives us to succeed and any time it is not controlled with human intuition, it will bring destruction. Self-compassion, an extension of outward passion, is also an important part of this practice.

How you perceive others is always through your own truth, even if it is tempered by a kind heart. Leave how you think others might be or not be suffering. Perceiving suffering is focusing on illusionary lack; it leads to nothing. Instead, focus on compassionately loving yourself and having the capacity to purely love all others no matter what arises.

This practice should bring to light your own story and afford you an ability to own it, face your fears and step up to meet life itself with full reverence.

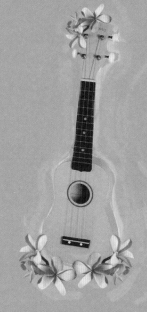

be pleased with yourself, very, very
pleased, play with yourself, explore
yourself, do as you please, delight
in yourself, you needn't explain yourself,
fall head over heels in LOVE with

give
yourself
a big
hug,
say
often,
I LOVE
YOU!"
to yourself

Hmmmm

your
true
self,
get
utterly
fascinate
in your
true
self.

be full of yourself, laugh with
give yourself   if you are not full
permission to   of yourself what
have fun.   are you full of?
over flow yourself onto the world.

selfish:
- putting oneself first,
- taking the lead role in the movie that is your life.
- Acting from an empowered, heart-opened, joyous energetic state of self love.
- Ecstatic love and compassion for self.

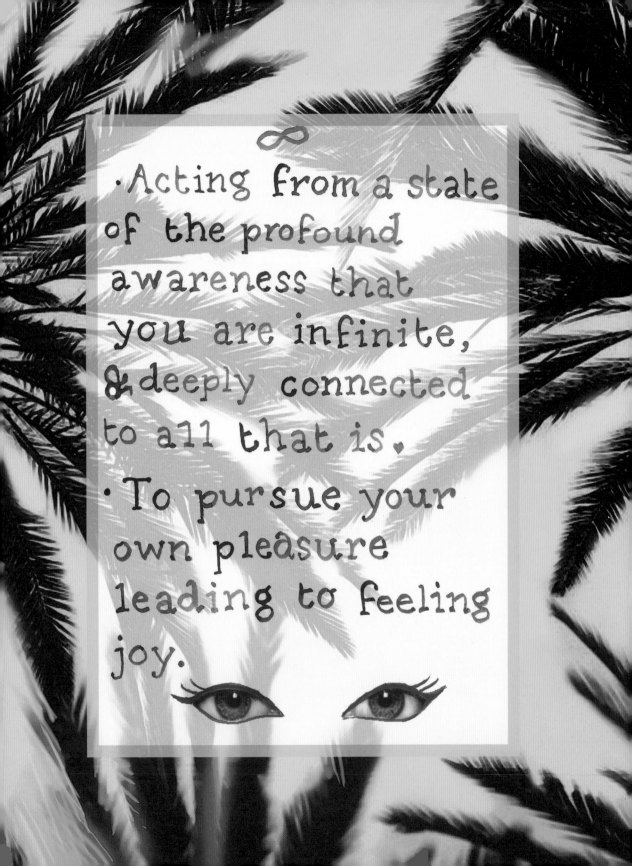

∞

· Acting from a state
of the profound
awareness that
you are infinite,
& deeply connected
to all that is.

· To pursue your
own pleasure
leading to feeling
joy.

seven graces

seven
virtues
diligence
temperance
patience
Chastity

Charity
kindness
Humility

Counsel
Courage
wisdom
discernment
knowledge
Wonder

Humble
devotion

re-birthing with self-love

Our third dimensional bodies are a slower frequency of energy so that they can be perceived by our senses.

Energy in motion (emotions) is fourth and fifth dimensional energy. Your eyes may not be trained to see multi-dimensional energy, just in the way that you generally don't see love, but you can feel this subtle energy and it deeply affects everything in your denser, third dimensional body.

On the 120th day of existing in the womb, soul light (subtle energy) is brought into the unborn baby's body. This soul light is diffused into a rainbow of self-expression through seven main energy vortices in the body, also known as the Chakras. The Chakras, often depicted as lotus flowers, transmute or transform energy throughout a person's life. How you perceive the world around you, and how you receive and transmute energy is affected by the openness of your Chakras.

Your past-life experiences and soul's strength determine the longitude and latitude of your birth here, and how open your Chakras are set at this time. After birth, your experiences through life also affect the openness of your Chakras. For example, if your Throat Chakra is less open at birth, how you communicate and relay your true Self with the world is affected from day one of your life. This can create further blockages until you are wise enough to heal the root cause. As each Chakra relates to a soul lesson, understanding your full birth chart and potential blockages in your Chakras will empower you to take command of your growth and self-healing. Understanding the challenges your soul chose for this life also affords greater self-compassion, which helps open your heart. With self-awareness, you can work to clear your Chakras and unlock your natural talents held in each energy centre. This rebirthing requires self-loving and patience. Just as a mother gives birth to a baby, you cannot force what is not ready without causing harm. Only a loving, self-empowered and enjoyable journey can lead to a loving and happy place, and all self-aggression must be dropped.

a golden age for soul growth

As heavenly portals increasingly open up there is greater potential to connect with your inner soul. As above, so below; as without, so within.

The past 12 000 years have been a heavy time that caused frustration and anger, due to a vague awareness of the entrapment of repeating cycles. Our feeling of victimhood escalated when we were born into the next life with very similar dramas. Little to no awareness of our own past 'miss-takes' meant that we put on our expected costumes and played familiar roles again and again.

The increased awareness flowing through the planet in this age will only lead to improvements if we are gentle and kind. It's vital to forgive yourself and love yourself with every new awareness that comes, so you can face your life, adjust to make improvements and move on. As you become aware of patterns of behaviour that no longer serve you, a self-loving approach will help you to work on positive change. This is a great time for connection, and the more we accept the help and love of others, the happier our healing journey.

This Aquarian Age is something that you need to experience yourself. This will take courage and a willingness to embrace new self-knowledge and a different perspective on life. It will require inner work and conversations with your soul. Trust your soul is ready, waiting to connect and guide you through each moment.

Your soul has great wisdom and knowledge gained from the past and future and, in this way, there is nothing more conscious than you. Your own soul is your own portal of light that you can connect with to learn everything relevant to your prosperity in the now. Your soul is your inner guidance system and, in alignment, you will feel whole and bright. As you grow in positivity, as you serve a higher purpose, your soul grows within you, which feels very complete and like being at 'home' in your experiences.

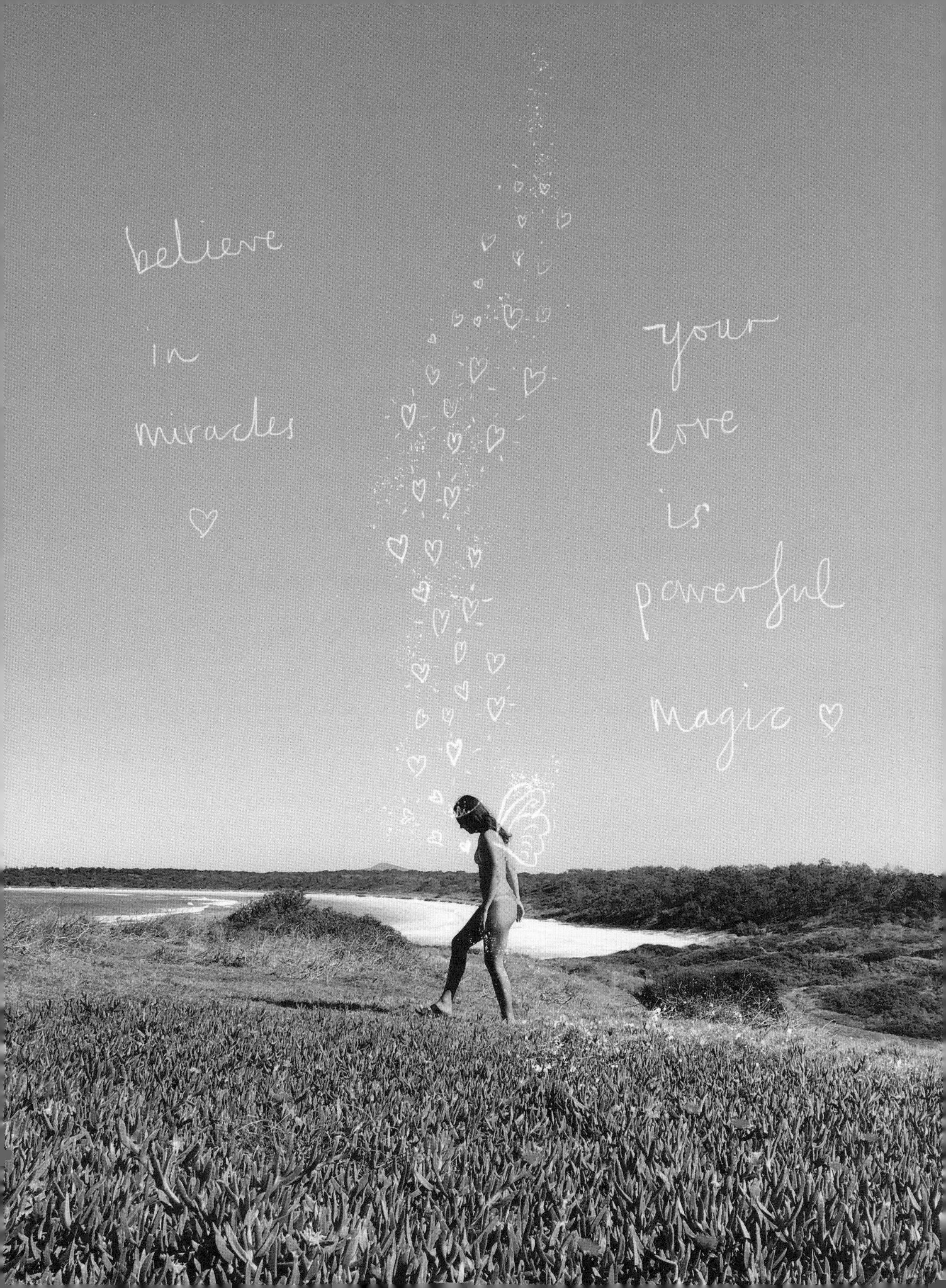
believe
in
miracles
♡
your
love
is
powerful
magic ♡

being the light of your soul

Everything that has ever been created comes from one source of non-divisible light energy.

This energy, also called 'God' and 'Source', created your soul by making a unique sound/vibration. Your soul's infinite journey is for the self-realisation of your uniqueness. *You are like no other.*

Your experience in this form is the result of 30 trillion points of the light of your soul manifested into a human blueprint.

When you open your heart and invite your soul to be expressed through every aspect of your being, you will open to your own unique sound, which can be felt as beautiful, worthy potential. In meditation practices that use sound, you are hunting and listening for the healing sounds that you make that resonate in harmony with your soul. Sounds you make that are in alignment with your soul are the most powerful, healing sounds for you to experience.

When you choose to ask your soul, 'Who am I?', 'What might I become?', 'What is the next right action?', and then listen to the answer, you are inviting more of the light (information) of your soul into your being. This subtle fifth dimensional energy holds a stream of answers for your body, heart and mind to be well and prosper. The light of your soul will give you an ability to see around the corners and blockages of the mind. And as the energy of the higher dimensions is increasingly streamed through the planet, the connection between the non-physical (your soul, other spirits and source) and the physical (your mind and body) will grow stronger.

The light of your soul appears as white light, and just as white light is made of a rainbow of colours, so is your soul. These hues of the rainbow are filtered through your Chakras in your subtle body. Through the Chakras, your soul's unique qualities colour your experiences and perceptions of each moment, in reality. The clearer your Chakras, the more of the light of your soul and your true Self can be embodied and fluidly expressed.

subtle nature

All the energy of the Universe lies within you and you have the power to master its subtle nature.

Your spiritual journey is very personal; your experiences cannot be compared to anyone else's or even to what you went through yesterday. The deeper you connect with your true Self, the less your Self has to do with anyone else and the closer you become to your own subtle nature. Only you can know your soul, the true nature of your own rhythmic intelligence, and only you can expand this energy within you. The open heart space is what should guide you on this journey; only you know what this feels like and when it is aligned with your soul. When you elevate yourself to live inspired (in-spirit) from this heart space to be who you truly are, you can serve others without resentment or hypocrisy.

The Aquarian Age invites you to understand the subtle nature of the Universe and how it interacts with your experience, so you can relax and enjoy each day.

Energies have been studied, experienced and understood by humanity for thousands of years, yet subtle energy is still not widely understood in many modern cultures.

As humanity evolves we will collectively increase our understanding of the true nature of all life, including the subtle realms of existence.

Ancient yogic science perceives human beings as made of the tattvas, which include the five elements of earth, water, fire, air, and ether. The quality of our lives, our minds, and our health is maintained by the tattvas. The human experience is also understood as having 10 bodies: the physical body, three mental bodies, and six energy bodies. The 11th embodiment comes when all 10 bodies are under pure conscious direction – the intention of becoming a yogi. There are 72 000 currents or nadis, which emanate from the navel point and end in the hands and feet. It is through these that the prana is carried to all the parts of the body. Each subtle fifth dimensional vibration and third dimensional form of the human being is intertwined with and affected by the other. The joy of this journey is in experiencing this brilliant design in unison.

Keep well hydrated
only wash your face with cold water
Use only organic products on your face.
fear, terror, panic, frustration, dread...
sorrow, shock, ungrateful, nervousness...
bladder
small intestine
bladder
anger, despair, boredom, passiveness...
gall bladder
gall bladder
LET GO + RELAX
heart
heart
self doubt, broken hearted, low self esteem...
Anger, rage, blame, bitterness
liver
liver
liver
ears Kidneys
ears Kidneys
envy, rejection, alienation...
Kidneys
Kidneys
anxiety, fear, paraniod, indecisive
criticism, doubt, greed, disappointment...
Stomach
pancreas
stomach
heart
rub noses to connect hearts
Rest with an eye pillow
lungs
lungs
small intestine
colon
colon
depression, predjuce, contempt...
hormonal balance..
endocrine system
guilt, grief, regret, sadness, shame...
heal with gratitude
large intestine
large intestine
for every experience
let go
Different emotions are stored in different organs and parts of the body.
Aestah Eltah, heal together.
darling, let go
gently massage your face to relieve tension from your whole body. Be gentle, be nourished
What is your face telling you?

you are made of 10 bodies

Our 10 bodies are a brilliant tool of self-realisation when led by the warmth of our heart.

1. soul body

The soul body is your beautiful infinite self, the vibration that you are, incarnate to be realised, the greatness that is your truth. You didn't come here to prove your greatness – you came to enjoy it.

2. negative mind

This protective energy at its best is intuitive, discerning and helps your dreams to take form and foresee potential pitfalls. Ensure your Third Eye is open so fear of the future, or only seeing problems, doesn't block you from seeing opportunities.

3. positive mind

The positive mind is an expansive energy with good humour and enthusiasm for infinite possibilities. This hopeful, positive mind can be overwhelmed by one's dominant, negative mind. Strengthen the Solar Plexus to stay empowered and keep the heart open for courage. If the positive mind is too strong, it can lead you and others astray into foolish ways. Its vibrant energy can block intuitive caution.

4. neutral mind

In this mind you are steady – not being endlessly swayed from negative to positive. Acting from a balanced mind leads to happiness and an ability to be your true Self and able to hold space for equilibrium – such as for yin and yang – and integrate all knowledge and wisdom through true perception.

5. physical body

When we feel safe and comfortable in our physical body we are not obsessed with its appearance; rather, we maintain a glowing grace and we embody divine energy and allow life to flow through us.

As we mature, we learn to value this temporary temple and respect its impermanence.

When balanced, we use our body to create, love, touch and deeply feel each moment. We serve and inspire all we meet, and teach others what we have come to understand through our experiences.

6. arc line body

The halo of your existence is the connection between Heaven and Earth, through you. The Arc Line (picture a halo that extends from ear to ear above your head) holds the Akasha (the records of everything you have ever done or said) and needs to be cleared regularly. Keep your Third Eye open to balance this energy. Be open to hearing guidance and willing to take appropriate action.

7. auric body

This is the electromagnetic field that surrounds your body. It projects and interacts with the energetic life force. It is your charisma and platform for expansive experiences for self-realisation.

8. pranic body

The infinite energy of the prana is the subtle spark of life carried on the breath.

It is our living connection to the infinite. Purity and fearlessness are experienced when this energy flows freely. Through this energy we can self-initiate, balance and integrate polarities.

9. subtle body

This subtle body energy holds the imprint of your journey – past, present and future.

Connecting to this energy creates knowing tranquillity. The unseen is seen, and the unknown can be known with mastery. Long-term consequences of actions and events can be foreseen.

10. radiant body

By reclaiming your human sovereignty, you can realise your radiance, nobility and totality. You can become a brilliant creator of magnificent reality. Through devotion to your true Self, you can find the courage to be creative, regardless of any obstacle or fear, and you will exceed all your expectations.

▽△▽

And then what of the 90 per cent of your mind? What can you become when you activate aspects of yourself that are dormant? What can you masterfully change for the betterment of all, in a heartbeat? Can you be still and draw the Universe into the palm of your hand to shift the course of the future beyond the fears that limit you?

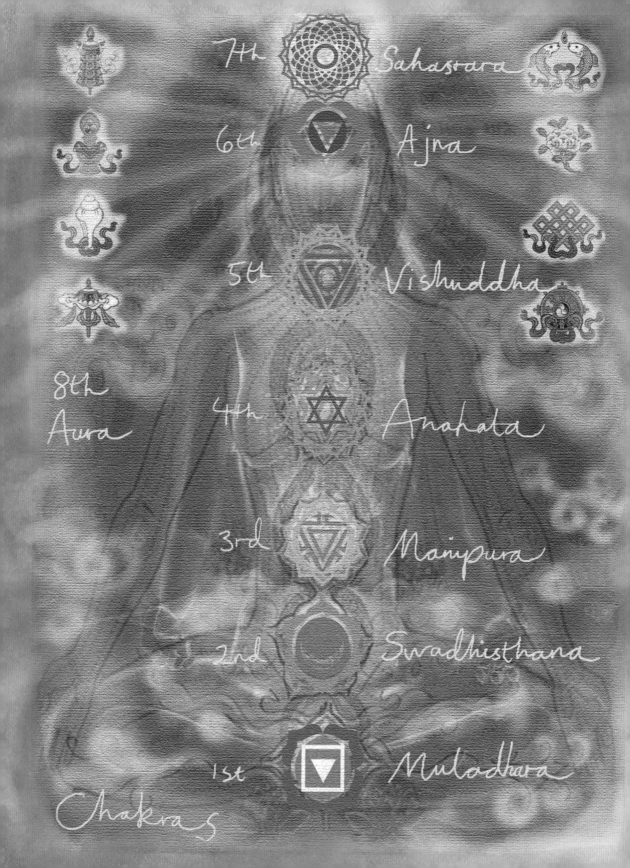

7th   Sahasrara

6th   Ajna

5th   Vishuddha

8th
Aura

4th   Anahata

3rd   Manipura

2nd   Swadhisthana

1st   Muladhara

Chakras

the chakras

All of your Chakras need to be clear and engaged, to manifest the life of your dreams.

The word Chakra comes from the Sanskrit word meaning 'wheel' or 'disc'. You may visualise these discs spinning and vibrating as the prana (cosmic energy/life force) moves through them. It is also helpful to think of the Chakras as gears – ultimately you want to be able to change gears, up and down the Chakras, for your health. Healthy Chakras that are clear and balanced, with energy flowing through them, help you to maintain good health, a sense of harmony and clear direction in life.

The Chakra system correlates to the major glands of the endocrine system. A balanced endocrine system, which governs your hormones, has a direct effect on your emotions and thoughts as well as your physical health. You can look at the Chakra system as a mapping of how the mind and body intersect and how your emotions live and intersects in your body, too.

The Chakra system is a developmental psychology, from the base of your spine to the crown of your head; from the most basic, foundational aspects of who you are, to the more advanced, subtle and skilful aspects of who you are. The normal cycle of life has different phases of development; there are different rites of passage that you go through in your energetic life and different skill-sets you develop and refine. Any major trauma, abuse or injury at certain phases of your development, has an effect on your subtle energy body. This also includes being subject to environmental toxicity, a poor diet, stress and worry.

The Chakras are active all the time, but at certain stages in one's life, different Chakras become the rite of passage. When you work with one Chakra, you are working with them all. These centres are each part of a whole.

The eight main Chakras are:.

Root Chakra, 0-7yrs

Sacral Chakra, 8-14yrs

Solar Plexus Chakra, 15-21yrs

Heart Chakra, 22-28yrs

Throat Chakra, 29-35yrs

Third Eye Chakra, 36-42yrs

Crown Chakra, 43-49yrs

Aura, from birth

a journey of self-love
with strength and courage

muladhara, root chakra

Muladhara *(mul = base, adhara = support)*

Location: *perineum, below genitals,*

base of the spine, the pelvis plexus

Related function: *adrenals, fight/flight response*

Associated body part: *bones, skeletal structure*

Bija mantra: *LAM*

make a wish

as you awaken from a deep sleep

love everything that arises....

Your innocent shadow self is no longer separated from your own consciousness & your deepest desires are realised as you love your whole-self unconditionally♥

I AM perfect.

fear Vs security

Your first Chakra is connected to the earth element and is related to your basic survival and safety needs.

The Root Chakra relates to how you see yourself in your surroundings. Before you were born, the orientation of this energy centre determined how your first needs were met. Your nervous system and breathing patterns were developed in the womb and inherited from your mother. You choose your birth mother in order to attune your frequency to attract certain soul lessons into your life. Everything in this life is synchronised and orchestrated on your behalf so that divine energy can be realised through you. However, trauma in the first seven years of life can lead to an individual believing the ego and the negative mind, which later leads to the belief that we are a victim of circumstance. Fortunately we are able to raise our awareness up through this Chakra toward the Solar Plexus — our seat of personal power. Any childhood wounds stemming from the heart and soul, such as struggling to be heard and nurtured, can cause a blind anger in our heart.

The colour red is associated with this Chakra and it relates to essential energy, blood, ancestry, passion and the foundation of Earth. As you spiritually mature, inherent and conditioned fears are replaced with the security of knowing yourself and trusting in your ability to manifest what your heart and soul desire. With a belief that you are supported by the Universe, along with practising self-honouring, your reality incrementally improves and allows your body to relax and the heart to soften. When you feel more secure within yourself, you will feel you are at 'home', and you will also connect to your surroundings in each moment. This feeling of being present in the real moment is where you will find all the energy of life. As destructive, fiery passion in the heart dissolves, a creative passion to succeed through service to others will arise. When you are no longer triggered like a red rag to a bull by life's challenges, you will attract better opportunities. A grounded presence ensures you are open to make the most of these opportunities, which may lead to security.

soul lesson: trust

Trust that only you know what is right for you and it is your birthright to experience ecstatic love – of yourself and life itself.

The biochemistry of joy releases an ambrosial nectar. This glandular secretion creates feelings often called ecstatic love. The Islamic practice of Sufism is well acquainted with ecstatic love. Sufis meditate through spinning, dancing and chanting in a way that leads to this ecstasy. Their poetry is woven with the concept of this state of blissful being.

You too can arrive at this state of inner bliss, through practising various styles of meditation. Meditation is not a luxury or just for spiritual masters, it is a necessary aspect of wellbeing in this expansive Aquarian Age. One of the reasons that a practice of self-honouring meditation is so important is that it will build an inner self-trust that will keep you steady and resilient in times of great change.

Life creates moments, and these moments become memories, which hold valuable lessons, when they are retraced. When these soul lessons are too strong they can be very heavy on the psyche. In childhood, lessons that caused fear make an imprint. Add to these the lessons of seven past generations you were born with (based on the yogic understanding of the cycles of lifetimes – memory passed from womb to womb) and you have an energetic block and distorted perception. It is challenging to trust the present moment if the chaos of distorted perception interferes. In each moment, your inner child, your confused adolescent, and your 254 ancestors affect your perspective and presence. Ancient wisdom and lessons are wonderful, but the inherent fears and neuroses can be debilitating. No one in your past has better answers to your questions than your inner wisdom. You are at the leading edge of new moments that pertain only to you. With a meditative mind, you can clear the past and get to know the real YOU. In a focused state of awareness, you will feel grounded and secure, capable and strong, and you will then trust yourself to take the next right action.

sense: smell

Your sense of smell is your strongest and first developed sense.

Smell belongs to primitive survival; animals rely upon it to survive in the wild. Smell responds faster than the other senses; smell correlates to your powerful, instinctive, emotional guidance system. Olfaction is a primal aspect of your sensory system: when you inhale aromatic molecules, they are instantly integrated into your body via your nasal passages and olfactory bulb, to the limbic region at the centre of the brain. The limbic centre is where all your emotions and memories are stored. It also regulates memory, creativity, motivation and the autonomic nervous system.

New associations can be created in your brain with aromatherapy – inhaling and applying the pure, organic, essential oils from plants. Essential plant oils can alter your mood, shift your perspective, deeply relax your mind and body, and assist you to let go of the past. When you breathe in the molecules of essential oils (plant vibrations), they have the ability to bypass the cerebral cortex, or the 'thinking part' of the brain, and give you access to your rhythmic intelligence, reminding you of your true Self. Aromatherapy works to release held trauma because the intelligence of plants communicates with the language of love, reminding your cells to expand and release old energy patterns. Preferably use only organic, non-GMO, pure essential oils as these offer the highest vibrational benefits and support appropriate farming practices. Use sweet almond, jojoba or camellia oil to dilute first if your skin is sensitive. These oils are also great to use for massage. Avoid contact with your eyes and sensitive skin areas; if by chance you get an essential oil somewhere sensitive, use a gentle oil like jojoba, camellia or sweet almond to remove it first (as like attracts like), then wash with cold water once the essential oil has been removed enough to reduce the sensitivity.

practice:

Inhale essential oil to add enthusiasm from your heart and inspiration from your soul. As you breathe out, surrender your vision to the Universe. Trust that everything always works out better than you could imagine.

element: earth

The more you connect with Mother Earth, the more complete you will feel.

The concept of lack doesn't exist outside of the human mind and this experience manifests when we aren't properly connected to Earth. We can be healed as we come into full awareness of our greater relationships. Earth is our true mother – we are made from her elements; she always supports us, and she lovingly and beautifully provides abundance. Mother Nature, not Earth, governs karma and it is our relationship with the Laws of the Universe that can block prosperity.

In our third-last breath of life we see everything we have lived flash before us; in our second-last, we have full awareness of what was intended to be realised; and in our last, we reflect upon this. If we condemn or are unforgiving toward ourselves, or we acknowledge we have not had reverence for the lives of others, we may ask that in the next life we are again given the opportunities to improve.

We may choose our own birth mother to present an aspect of our shadow Self that we wish to heal, particularly relating to our ongoing relationship with the divine feminine. As a child this can be challenging, but as we mature we can choose to change our attitude toward ourselves and heal this wound. We are always given immense Universal support to move through any chosen lessons. Our relationship with our birth mother can also reflect past fears that Earth wasn't supportive in our past life. However, when we trust and purify our intentions around this planet's resources, we can receive the prosperity we have dreamt about. To foster a deep, healing connection with Mother Earth, we need to listen to Her story, Her wisdom, and keep learning. When we can acknowledge and unpack the inherited and collectively held fears and lies, the joy in realising that Earth has always loved humanity brings solutions, opportunities and abundance.

Every day, for at least three minutes, if you stand barefoot on natural grass, bare earth, sand or rock, you will receive great benefits to open this Root Chakra and your heart.

and
the
elementals
beckon
you to
go deeper,
lost in
simply
being
♡

Kali is the Hindu goddess of yogic transformation.

Kali's bija mantra is KRIM

Meditate upon her image & yantra for freedom from ego.

Clear, strong & truth in the present.

Kali is above and beyond all concepts of good & evil, positive & negative. She is very loving and motherly to all that is reality. She brings the death of the ego as the illusory view of reality. Call upon Kali to fearlessly liberate your soul from ego attachments.

energy: warrior

Through self-love you can access the full power of your life force.

When you view yourself as a peaceful warrior of change, you open this Root Chakra to the tremendous energy that breathes within you.

A peaceful warrior desires harmony and acknowledges that shame and guilt are negative responses to valuable Earth lessons. True warriors do not blame others; instead they seek unity and acknowledge that we are all in this moment together. As you enter the energetic space of the peaceful warrior, you practise shaping your physical body with the power of your mind, understanding that the psycho-emotional state must be harnessed and focused on being of service.

A warrior doesn't separate themselves or others into good or evil, rather they see everything as a whole. In others' reflections they see what needs to be loved and healed within themselves. Warriors go within to find wisdom in their open heart and have the capacity to love beyond boundaries. Seeing the interconnectedness of everything, warriors picture themselves in all others – large and small. To the warrior, true liberation is Heaven meeting Earth.

A warrior practises alchemy and seeks to merge masculine and feminine energies on a spiritual and physical level.

Through the female womb, the deep mystery of all life is birthed and rebirthed. A warrior understands that the sexual, earthly feminine energy must be surrendered to and adored by all for there to be ongoing life, peace and harmony.

Peaceful warriors tame 'dragons' for the benefit of all. The dragon is symbolic of the combined elemental powers of the Earth, and by befriending and understanding these forces one is empowered. Ancient Eastern myths inform us that rather than conquering and slaying the 'dragon', we prosper through reverence and appreciation for the elemental forces.

Warriors acknowledge, 'Earth my body, Water my blood, Air my breath, Fire my spirit, Ether my soul light'. They know that they only need to harness the power of the Universe within their flesh and bones to be peacefully victorious over destructive forces.

Now is the time to express the divine
feminine in each and every aspect
where it lies locked beneath inherent
fears.
Let us surrender to the fullness, the
ripeness, the creativity and divine
flow of life force within.
Surrender to embracing pleasure.
Curves, spirals, softness, warmth
and fragrance of the abundant
feminine energies.
May we allow ourselves to unite with
our true selves, our complete self,
our other aspects found in the yin
And only known to taste as sweet
by contrast to the yang.
With gratitude for the yang, the
nectar of the yin is ripe for release.
The primordial juices flow once again
We connect with soul mates and
in gratitude for experiencing guilt
we open to truest pleasures.

Now we let go of that which no longer
serves us, only seeds of wisdom retained.
And these seeds are now sown in
fertile soil and attended to only with love.
For it is now, only in love that we create,
that we co-create a true garden of Eden.
Vows of old and ancient ways sent to
no-thing from whence they came.
Self sacrifice, guilt in pleasure, fear in
illusions~ all vanished.
The waters be still and as the full
moon rises we see the truth in our reflections.
We are love, we are perfect, we are abundant,
we are cherished, we are supported, we are
infinite beings who once believed we were
separate and now this innocence is replaced
with the knowing of our true divine nature.
In celebration we unite, we grow and expand.
Unimaginable pleasures are experienced and
our existence known by no measure of limit.

the gift of freedom

When you choose to lay down your weaponry of self-harm and self-judgement, you will find freedom.

In doing so, you will free others. The gift of this energy centre is to find the freedom of comfort in your own body and see it as a safe and divine temple. Your physical body has been intelligently designed to be a vehicle to express creation. Listen to your body and know when to move and when to rest. Develop your physical body so you can go and get what you want. If you do this, you will also notice that everything you desire will come to you. When you look after yourself you build an inner trust that creates a trust in the greater Universe. As you begin to feel the grace of existence coming through your body, you are freed from attachment to Maya (material).

A very simple way of opening up the flow of energy in the Root Chakra is to explore dancing with loving abandon, led by your heart. Dance away your doubt and be the authority that says yes to fun. Your brain experiences information in the rhythm of a logical 4/4 beat. The rhythmic intelligence in your heart experiences the same information at 3/4 beat. So listen to your heart and allow your feet and body to be guided in a moving meditation. When you feel the freedom of this, you will be touching the continuum of existence. No longer just feeling the crude logic of your surroundings, your meditative mind will serve you to find freedom and joy in self-expression. When you dance with life and disappear into its continuous rhythm you will be free of illusions and entranced by your own magic. When this happens, there is no more distinction between upper and lower areas of the body. You become just one flow of energy, and the kundalini (awareness) will awaken and dance up your spine, creating an elevated state.

May your continuous journey of self-love begin from this heightened, open, receptive and grounded place, finding the freedom to feel the full embodiment of your true Self in every cell.

plant wisdom

By eating foods that keep our bloodstreams and terrains clean, the Earth will experience the same vibrant health.

When you become more relaxed, you do not deplete your own 'Jing' essence. But if the 'Jing' essence is depleted it can trigger a primal survival instinct, which can lead to seeking 'fast' food.

Eating the flesh of another animal has been perceived since the Ice Age as necessary to survive and replenish 'Jing'. However, your 10 bodies can be completely nourished, sustained and renewed by eating from just the plant kingdom. As you absorb the vibrations of everything that you consume, a plant-based diet is a natural choice for healing and lifting your vibration. If an animal has died in fear, it holds that fearful energy in its flesh, organs and blood. You become the energy you absorb and generate. Herbivores are sharing animals; carnivores are territorial, aggressive and competitive. When carnivorous races dominated and claimed ownership of Earth, humanity fell into a hypnosis of ignorance. In the Aquarian Age, as we share our awareness of what is fair, we begin to surrender to the heart of peace. Healthy humans living on plant-based diets are providing inspiration and evidence that this is the evolutionary path to a better future. A balanced, organic, plant-based diet can be easily assimilated and offers the mind, body and soul complete nourishment, which leads to abundance and good health.

We actually thrive on the simplest of energetic relays (relay-tionships), with beauty, nature, sound and positive vibes. Being grounded through your full presence and being seated when you eat, loving yourself and blessing the food you eat and the planet it comes from, is to live in harmony. The Aquarian Age asks that we change our habits in ways that make better use of energy and heal the Self and the planet together. Growing, foraging and harvesting plant foods, and also purchasing directly from growers and producers, will open your Root Chakra and bring you closer to inner peace and joy.

Blessings
Ganesha
for removing
all obstacles
on my
path.

I pledge
to be who I AM
no matter what

sensual therapy

smell

Pure essential oils to work with the Root Chakra (please use high-quality organic product): vetiver, black pepper, frankincense, ylang-ylang, cedarwood, fennel and patchouli. Use single oils or create a blend. **Oil applications:** inhalation, sacrum, back of neck, bottom of feet, little toe, pinky finger.

taste

Hibiscus tea is a beautiful deep-red herbal tonic that destroys spiritual and material obstacles, purifies the physical and spiritual heart, promotes wisdom and assists in realising goals. This tea is also a kidney, reproductive organ, skin and hair tonic, and can be enjoyed throughout the day, served warm or cold.

touch

Crystals to use with the Root Chakra:
Balancing – Red Jasper
Soothing – Tourmaline
Stimulating – Red Garnet

sound

A mantra to strengthen the Root Chakra is the Mul mantra, literally the 'Root mantra', which eliminates fear. (See resources).

intuition

Practise Sat Kriya for 3–31 minutes every day. Amazing results and shifts are experienced by practising this exercise consistently over a long period of time. (See resources).

affirmations

I AM HERE

I AM COURAGEOUS

I AM GROUNDED

I AM SUPPORTED

I AM OF THIS EARTH

I AM RESPECTFUL

I HAVE APPROPRIATE BOUNDARIES

I AM FREE TO BE ME

ritual: honouring cycles

You came to Earth to connect with the richly creative tapestry of life and to weave your colours through it.

When you connect to Earth and its cycles and rhythms, you are connecting with the gifts of change, here to serve your expansion. The crystalline grid of Earth, the Song lines, the elements, the Moon cycles, the seasons, the days, are present to offer experiences. When you align with Earth's cycles, the next right action becomes clearer and the results are more potent.

Each solstice and equinox offers huge potential for shifts in awareness, release from the past, deep healing and energetic activation. The less-frequent solar and lunar eclipses offer exponential opportunity for evolution. The planets that transit Earth circulate energy through this time-space to stretch and shape every individual's reactions and responses to life. Understanding these cycles in relation to your natal chart offers great insights for opening and healing the Chakras. The seasons create a cycle, starting with birth at spring, to summer celebration, with autumn letting go and the death of winter. Opportunities to grow, shed, rebirth, to accept and enjoy the temporary nature of life are offered.

Each day of the week is also aligned and energised with different planets. Every seven days you have energetic support to manifest your dreams.

Monday, Moon:

Emotion, reflection and rest.

Tuesday, Mars:

Extroversion, energy and combativeness.

Wednesday, Mercury:

Business and communication.

Thursday, Jupiter:

Expansion and deep thought.

Friday, Venus:

Love, sensuality, home and career.

Saturday, Saturn:

Karma, completion, work and discipline.

Sunday, Sun:

Purity, energy of the Self, joy and play.

lay down all your weapons of self harm.

Be honest, listen, hear your thoughts, embrace kindness.

You no longer judge yourself, you accept yourself fully & purify your thoughts.

illuminate

I am the light of my soul. Connect with the fire element to purify.

I am beautiful, I am bountiful I am bliss. I AM, I AM.

PURE JOY

too fat too thin not slow too ugly poor loud hungry sad dont cant shut eat they shouldnt up dont bad like yuk blah you blah blah

Light a candle and gaze at the light, the flame soften, relax, connect with your heart.

Keep your oil in a bottle and label it with the energy you want to absorb.

massage

reveal and nurture the beauty within ♡

Using organic sweet almond oil give yourself a full body massage, starting with the feet, massage up towards the heart. circular strokes around joints, long strokes along limbs, then hands, up the arms and to the shoulders towards the heart, then torso, breasts, face, scalp & hair.

love self massage every day

surrender

Waterfall, stream, ocean, shower, bath, rain, connect with the water element, release and let go of everything.

release + wash away

Wash off in cold water, using the same motion, rub until each body part is warm.

This is so good for your whole being ♡

blissful ♡

Do one 'section' under the water at a time ♡

you are pure love bless yourself often.

Cacao butter

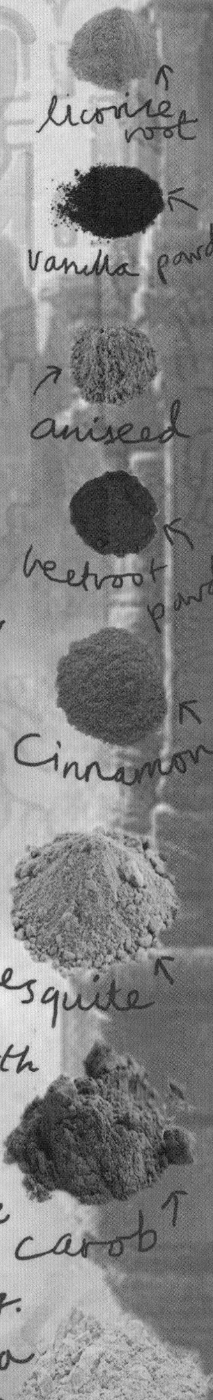

licorice root

vanilla powder

aniseed

beetroot powder

cacao liquor

Cinnamon

Coconut nectar sugar

Enjoy this drink
with good company,
fill the room with
the aroma of this
beautiful drink
and bring in all the
elements to connect
consciously to each
other and Mother Earth

Pink salt

black pepper

Mesquite

yum

EARTH: Cacao, plants
WATER: In the drink
FIRE: candles, incense
AIR: breath, music, singing.
ETHER: silence,
meditation,
contemplation.

carob

lucuma

ceremonial cacao

Ingredients:

100g cacao butter.

100g cacao liquor (aka, raw cacao paste or mass)

50g coconut sugar

1/4 tsp pink salt

pinch of pepper

2 tsp beetroot powder

1 tsp vanilla powder or essence

1 tsp ground liquorice root

3 tsp ground cinnamon

2 tbsp mesquite powder

2 tbsp carob powder

2 tbsp lucuma powder

Method:

Melt the cacao butter and liquor, coconut sugar, salt and pepper together in a large glass jug or bowl, in a 40-50 degree C oven. Stir about every 15 minutes over the hour or so it takes to melt.

Sift dry ingredients together in a bowl.

Stir into melted ingredients.

Add small amount of hot water for desired consistency.

Serves 3-6.

Pour or ladle into small bowls or cups of choice. Serve with love.

Thank Mother Earth and bless her and each other before drinking.

Ceremony

Having experiences of open-hearted connectedness to each other and Mother Earth is very important for feeling secure and at 'home'. Cacao is a gift to humanity, from the heart of nature, to awaken a deep connection to Mother Earth, Spirit and the oneness of all.

This sacred heart-opening food relaxes the brain yet doesn't remove us from consciousness; rather, it invites us to drop into our hearts. When we exist in our own heart space we can soften, relax and open to more love. We can have a rose-coloured view of our Self.

rooms and womb

I packed up my old house on the dark moon. As I shed and culled and cleansed and let go and released, Lilith herself sat on my shoulder and she was brutal. As I packed I thought about how many times I'd done this over the years, in Paris, NY, Sydney, Biarritz, Alice Springs, Fiji and how often I have reinvented myself. It is more tiring with three people's shit, even though I love this shedding, going over the fragments of myself, but there are many. The desert dweller's camp gear, the Parisian's wardrobe, the chapter when I was a wife. I am, have been them all. But these old love stories, old careers must only live in my memory now, there's literally no room for them here. One morning before brekkie in my uggies, I light a fire in the front yard and throw all these stories into it. Once I start, I can't stop. Mid-packing, a cheeky snake turns up in my bedroom, (thanks Lilith) it is high drama, involves kitchen tongs and a makeshift snake bag that I don't use and me screaming at the kids to get back while I hold this brown friend at arm's length until we get her outside, all the while she hisses at me. It's transformation time sister, leave the old right here to make way for the yummy newness, you're not taking that with you. How many parts of me have I already left behind I wonder, my personal story composting into fresh roots with the lands? What will feed my inner seedling in the new patch of earth? How much of the real me do I unpack for others to see? Do you know me? How much do I allow my possessions to possess me? Because our new place is so small (and can be swept in 3 mins flat) I ask what is important to me and my kids now. This list is small, has been refined over the years. The music, cameras, notebooks and salvaged art pieces and trinkets that travel with me are living stories. I give away most of our stuff, am ruthless. Fuck it's cleansing, my kids don't care. I think of it as downsizing to expand. We move in on the new moon, divine timing for a fresh start, but my life down here is like that, in natural rhythm with above. I wouldn't have it any other way. I get everything we need into half a truck and when I arrive before them, know I'm supposed to be here when I see the way the morning light hits the jarrah wood kitchen bench and think of my groms with bed head peeling boiled eggs early, the wood fire warming us, think of weekends with my lover leaning me up against it gently, sometimes roughly. When I take my first bath I see the moon and the stars peering in at me through the large window and when I sit on the back deck writing the first time, the way the west facing arvo light warms my fingers as I type and the two black cockatoos call and the bamboo creaks all around me, I know. This cabin with walls that only I decorated, shelves that I drilled by myself, utilities connected. All by me, every rock, chair, box lifted and unpacked by moi. This home that my father will never see. This new way sprouting wildly from inside of me. Here.

Carly Lorente (pictured opposite)

3rd dimension,
physical realm.
4th dimension
astral realm,
energy in motion
(E-motions).
together 3rd and
4th dimensions make
up the lower creation
world where the
game of separation
is played out.
5th dimension,
light body realm.
full awareness,
no good or evil,
united creative
energy & spiritual
orientation.

*a journey of self-love
flowing with creativity*

swadhisthana, sacral chakra

Swadhisthana (*swa = self or prana, dhisthana = dwelling place*)

Location: *the area 25mm to 50mm below the navel*

Associated body part: *sex organs, large intestine, appendix, lower vertebrae, bladder, hips*

Related function: *sexual, elimination, water regulation*

Bija mantra: *VAM.*

flow Vs stagnation

The Sacral Chakra is related to the element of water, and to procreation.

It is the centre of your creativity, desire, emotions, sexuality, and intuition. It is where you plant the seeds of creativity and learn to give and receive pleasure. This Chakra stimulates the life force, other forces required for existence on the physical plane and the base of life itself. Children from the ages of 8–14 belong in this Chakra. It is an age when we become established, which frees up time to explore friendships, sexuality and physical contact.

The Sacral Chakra is the pathway to health and youth. When it is open you will feel connected to everything. There will be a creative elegance to your accomplishments rather than a push to achieve. Insecurities around the true Self, sexuality, attractiveness, and feelings of inadequacy, shame and embarrassment can be stored in the Sacral Chakra. Healing work in this Chakra will release stagnant energy in the related areas of the body and will assist you to surrender to the creative flow of life. To create a flow of energy through this centre, you can work with the breath and movement, to raise the kundalini, from the base of the spine, opening the heart and bringing awareness into the higher centres. With increased awareness, you can see more clearly where you have judged or shamed yourself and then choose to only think about yourself very lovingly.

Working with mudras and mantras can help to change habitual negative thinking patterns, removing 'bad' thoughts that manifest as karma and increasing your ability to manifest your true desires. To heal childhood, adolescent and ancestral wounds, work on integrating and celebrating your uniqueness and all aspects of the masculine and the feminine within you. Know that you are blessed with both the mysterious and unique creative vision (female), and the ability to manifest with clarity in the physical plane (male). Keep hydrated and move the body to free up your hips and nourish your fluid, feminine (yin) aspects.

soul lesson: surrender

By surrendering your visions of pleasure to the Universe completely, you will give them the blessing of belief needed for them to actualise.

When you were young, the shame you experienced if you felt you hadn't succeeded directly affected your vulnerability. Shame is a basic human reaction to the concept of lack, and comes from the negative mind. In an attempt to avoid feeling shame, you may have blamed others for any discomfort and you may have avoided doing new things.

When you are self-protecting and self-loving, you realise that you get to choose your attitude, and you can allow yourself to do new things with an open heart and a neutral, calm mind. You encourage yourself to do things that offer you beneficial, and new, experiences. Through the courage of your heart, you are empowered to surrender your will to the things that support you, and move away from those that don't.

You know what is right for you and what gets your creative juices flowing. The sovereign path is to courageously follow your creative impulses for self-expression and realisation, without doubt or need for any outside approval.

By surrendering to the creative life force, you are not making yourself vulnerable – instead, you are unlocking a very powerful force within you. This creative force is unstoppable; it creates worlds, abundance and life itself. Moving the body in tight areas, like the hips and pelvis, whilst also opening the heart and Third Eye, works to free the mind from any self-limiting thought patterns and helps you find freedom.

When you surrender with movement to this primal force, the fear of 'getting it wrong' can be replaced with joy and an inner spaciousness that leads to liberated self-expression. Trust that the Universal energy that creates all life wants you to fulfil your creativity, and for good things to come back to you.

Shakti, power, is not outside of you.
You embody the currents of existence.
Adi Shakti, Adi Shakti, Namo Namo
I bow to the primal power, the first power,
feminine in its aspect, transcending the rational mind.

sense: taste

Taste is the sense associated with your second Chakra, and the action of giving and receiving pleasure.

Your true personal taste, which extends beyond tasting food, comes from your rhythmic intelligence. This vibrational orientation should not be ignored – it is your personal inner guide.

In a world where so many choices exist, knowing your subtle preferences that work to support your life can simplify your decisions. When any thought process is simplified, clarity comes and feels wonderful. Your personal taste encourages you to express who you are and enables you to confidently give and receive, because you know your true Self. This energy centre beckons you to go with the flow and slow down to enjoy everything that tastes nourishing. Rather than think about what you need, allow yourself to acknowledge the subtle signals your body sends you.

When you listen to your body, rather than your conditioned mind, you can be guided to eat intuitively. Mindful eating is a powerful pathway to good health. Listen for requests: your stomach may need a rest from eating, or you may need a specific food for healing or energy. Your sense of taste can be dulled when you are not fully engaged or present in the task of eating. Make space to enjoy and truly digest your food. Doing so will bring so much pleasure to your daily nourishment. By honouring your true energetic nature, you will replenish your energy in a precise way and serve your longevity. At mealtimes, eat smaller portions and chew each mouthful very well. It is very beneficial to chew each mouthful at least 20 times. Chewing your food thoroughly will aid digestion because the food will be fully coated in your saliva's digestive enzymes. Many plant foods are naturally very sweet and properly chewing your food will release this sweetness, which is very satisfying for the gut/mind. Remember your stomach doesn't have teeth and chewing in a relaxed way can relieve tension from your hips.

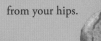

element: water

The element of water clears energy in the Sacral Chakra.

*Drink the pure water of this planet
and be energised.
Take pleasure in the sparkling oceans,
in the taste of the sea.
Enjoy sweat and tears, let energy flow.
Go to the mountains where the water
falls from high; absorb purity
and be replenished.*

drink

Drink more water and then some.
Enjoy every drop.

eat

Eat hydrating, watery fruits, like the ones that drip down your chin and fill your mouth with a burst of energy. Melons, especially, are Heaven-sent and a complete food for relaxing, hydrating and energising the body. Watermelons provide nourishment similar to human breast milk. If you were stranded on a desert island, watermelons could sustain you way better than bread and water. Cucumbers are another super food that cools and hydrates.

bathe

Add mineral salts to your bath to be energised. Be sure to keep hydrated.

cold showers

For a radiant glow have these every day or at least once a week. Or finish a warm shower with cold water. Cold water stimulates the blood in the internal organs to rush out to the surface of the skin. This cleanses and energises the glandular system. Move into or under the water one limb at a time and vigorously rub your skin. This helps you to develop grit and face your challenges, like a warrior.

swim, swim, swim

Swim in an ocean, river, lake, or any clean body of water. Do this at every opportunity. It seems obvious, but we often forget how good this feels.

sweat and cry

Every day, move until you sweat, and laugh until you cry. This will bring you gratitude, happiness and longevity.

the sacred art of making love

Connect, move everything and get the primordial juices flowing.

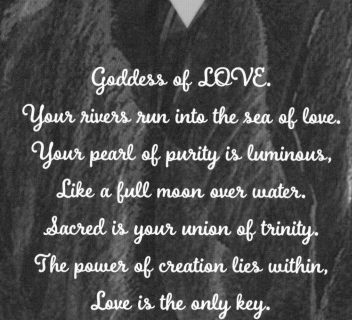

Goddess of LOVE.
Your rivers run into the sea of love.
Your pearl of purity is luminous,
Like a full moon over water.
Sacred is your union of trinity.
The power of creation lies within,
Love is the only key.
O CHICCA CHICCA
NA NA TOM

energy: warrior

Do not fear your power, your sexuality, or the mysterious ebbs and flows of your life.

Surrender to the mystery of life, control only your mind and become a master of your time. The Earth needs strong, creative warriors — humans in leadership who can work together to heal the planet.

What will you bloom into as the new Earth is realised? What wild and precious jewel is locked within your Sacral Chakra? What intriguing luminosity can you bring to the surface? When we unlock the energy in this centre we will find an amazing capacity for creativity and pleasure. As we learn to rise from the fear-based emotions of the lower Chakras and sustain our awareness in the heart, we can go even further to experience new depths of our creativity and our pleasure zones. Much of what we learn about our creative ability and bodies is through inappropriate comparisons. We are often taught from a young age what is not right about us; how not to express ourselves, how we measure up, how to suppress our feelings and many of our preferences. We are also taught that there is danger in being too different. So we tend to block sensations and deny our originality and deep desires.

Blocking your sacred energy can lead to disease. To be well, express every aspect aching to be realised. The Sacral Chakra warrior dives deep into the ocean of their true Self and their sexuality, freely exploring creative expression in every level of their life. They must ignore anyone who disapproves of them, and find a community that supports them. This warrior respects themselves and understands the importance of keeping a balanced life to preserve their Ojas. Ojas is said to be the pure substance that is accumulated from properly digested and nourishing food. It gives life and energy to the cells in the body, reduces signs of aging and protects against disease. A person with 'good' Ojas tends to have a healthy, luminous glow. They are patient and compassionate and rarely become sick.

the sacred art of making love

Dissolve all barriers to pleasure.

The sacred art of making love is not intended to be just physiological or emotional; it is intended to be a spiritual practice, where you actually make love and space for your expansion.

You will enjoy making love more if there is true polarity. Opposites are just two expressions of one energy – the yin and the yang. You can play out this polarity any way, but the magic will happen when you can fully embody the polarity and move through the peaks and valleys until you choose to unite the two halves. The practice of making love is an opportunity to invite more consciousness into your sexual experiences and then allow this awareness to flow into your life. Remember this is an opportunity to work with a very powerful energy, which can assist you to express your creativity, your true personality and manifest your desires.

The Throat Chakra (communication) and the Third Eye (intuition) are the first Chakras to engage.

Females benefit from being aroused for up to 72 hours prior to making love, to be fully open to the experience. Having a direct relay with your sexual partner is the beginning of making love. Speak your truths and be honest about the type of relationship you desire. This then becomes the container for the exploration of delight and celebration. Consciously breathing together as you gaze into one another's eyes will set the stage for a deep connection. Be present and open rather than goal-oriented; it is a fluid journey and interaction of souls in the physical and non-physical. Move slowly, massage each other, touch lightly, allow energy to open through your bodies and feel your hearts also opening into the experience. Women move energy from the inside to the outside and men from the outside to the inside. Go anywhere you agree to and when you come to a peak, breathe deeply and raise the energy from the base of your spine up to your crown and enjoy the feeling of it showering you with blessings. Focus the creative energy of this sacred union and use it to manifest what your heart desires. Rest in the sweet valleys – they are just as potent as the peaks, for transformation.

I give
myself
full
permission
to receive
pleasure.

the gift of creativity

Need? Create.

As we clean up the mess, with our human brothers and sisters, on this planet, what is real and what matters will shine through. We are divine, creative beings, each having the power of the Universe within us, ready to create great beauty. Our minds are very powerful tools and when we organise them to stop ourselves from complaining, self-doubting and being negative, prosperity reigns and our intelligence can be used for creativity.

Social changes due to advances in technology and connectivity will continue in leaps and bounds. In one moment, huge creative shifts can occur around the globe, that can counter any destruction. A relatively small shift on an individual level is magnified by a collective shift. For example, one person saying 'no' can seem insignificant, yet when 10 million individuals say 'no' at once this has a very large effect. As the past becomes obsolete, creative, new solutions for every way we live will emerge. Cruel practices against sentient beings are being peacefully petitioned to become non-existent. Peaceful marches are shifting the collective consciousness; start-ups and crowd funding are propelling whole generations into Aquarian entrepreneurship. These Soulpreneurs are inventing and creating new ways to responsibly consume, whilst bringing abundant health and wellbeing to themselves and the whole planet. It has been said that if humanity came together and in the same moment said 'I love you' with hands over their hearts, all the oceans would heal. You can be the alluring, mysterious individual that creatively changes and evolves. Stop paying attention to the opinions of others. Instead, inspire others to have the courage to shine the light of their souls, as their human duty.

Pictured opposite: Saraswati, Goddess of Creativity, bestows purity of creativity, knowledge and freedom from the Knot of Maya (material attachment).

plant wisdom

Taste the sweetness and ripeness in every moment as you live, seasonally attuned.

Each season's foods give your being signals to go with the flow and receive the pleasure of nourishment.

'All is well and relax; life is simple,' plant foods tell your body.

Eating a wide range of fresh fruits and vegetables is truly a preventative medicine because plants offer cleansing, protective and nourishing energy for the seasons to come. This way of eating rewards you, the animals and the planet.

A wise approach to eating each day is to imagine you were to gather food straight from an abundant garden from first thing in the morning (which is the ideal way to eat). What would you look for? You would most likely look for hydrating, sweet food, like ripe fruits, which can be a source of easily absorbed energy. For the meals later in the day, you may choose leafy greens and crisp vegetables. Denser, richer, and more grounding foods, like root vegetables, nuts

and seeds, would be sourced later as these foods take time to prepare.

When you find a kind and generous balance with your relationship to food, you can enjoy proper self-nourishment without denial or over-indulgence. Listen to the 'food' your heart and soul guides you toward. Every meal should be renewing, healing and satisfying. Follow the flow of seasons, moon cycles and your own different energy needs, so you can eat with awareness, and intuitively, without rules.

For this Chakra, the following sweet and watery foods promote healing, deep nourishment and youth: sweet potatoes, oranges, melons, mangoes, papaya, bananas, grapes, pineapples, berries, apples, cherries, water chestnuts and lotus root.

Unfurl like a beautiful flower to give and receive pleasure, and then become the one who tastes the sweet nectar of life.

plant sugars are
easily absorbed
by your
body,

calming
for the
nerves,

yum

fruits
are
mouthfuls
of sunshine
& joy.

yum

Relax,
you deserve
to be well
nourished
eat lots of fruit
each season.

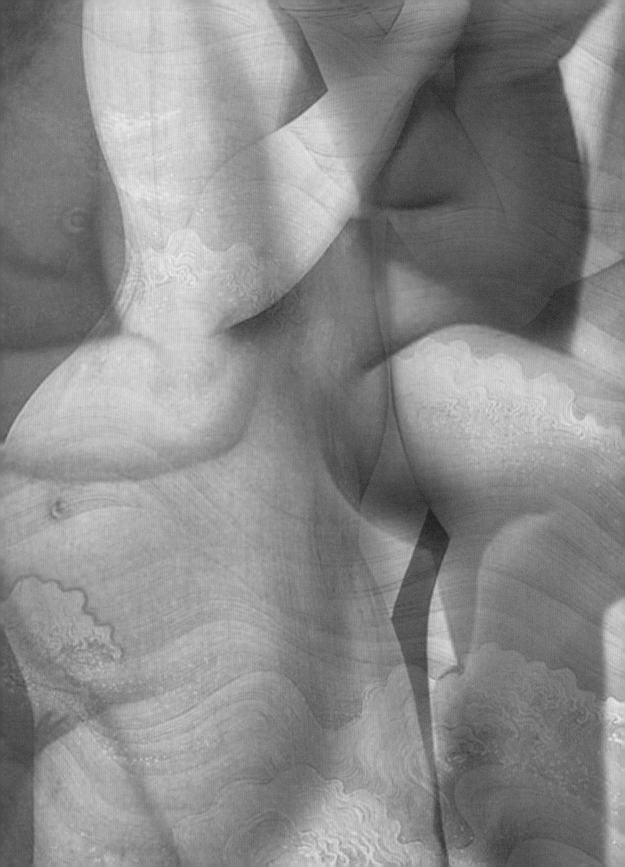

sensual therapy

smell

Pure essential oils to work with the Sacral Chakra (please use high-quality organic product): orange, clary sage, fennel, black pepper, bergamot, ylang-ylang, cardamom and rosemary. **Oil applications:** inhalation, bottoms of feet, navel area, ring toe and ring finger.

taste

Coconut nectar sugar is a nourishing and versatile wholefood sugar made from the evaporated nectar of coconut palm blossoms. Traditional communities refer to the coconut tree as the 'Tree of Life'. Producing an average of 50-75 per cent more sugar per acre than sugar cane, and using less than one fifth of the nutrients for that production, it has a well-deserved reputation as the planet's most sustainable sweetener. Coconut sugar contains iron, magnesium and zinc. It is a great tasting and low GI (35) sweetener.

touch

Crystals to use with the Root Chakra:
Balancing – Sun Stone
Soothing – Amber
Stimulating – Carnelian

sound

The mantra Ong Namo Guru Dev Namo has been translated as 'I bow to the creative energy of the Infinite: I bow to the Divine teacher within me'. It is also considered a mantra of protection. Focus your awareness at the area just below your navel while you repeat silently or aloud: Ong Namo Guru Dev Namo. (See resources).

affirmations

I AM CREATIVE

I AM CONNECTED

I FLOW WITH MY EMOTIONS

I AM YIN

I AM YANG

I AM BEAUTIFUL

I AM POWERFUL

ritual: aromatherapy and crystal bath

I am beautiful, I am bountiful, I am bliss, I am, I am.

Fill your bathtub with nice hot/warm water. While it fills, add bath salts:

1/3 cup pure magnesium salt flakes

1/3 cup epsom salts

1/3 cup bi-carbonate

Add the following blend of organic essential oils and mix:

5 drops of organic rose absolute diluted to 3 per cent in jojoba oil

5 drops of vanilla

2 drops of cardamom

1 drop of sandalwood

3 drops of ylang-ylang

2 drops of patchouli

Swish around the water to dissolve the salts and blend the oils.

Place quartz crystals in the bathtub (any you are drawn to, like rose quartz, smokey quartz, crystal quartz, etc.)

Light candles and place around bath. Candles in crystals are ideal.

Play this 31-minute mantra (repeat if desired:):

Dhan Dhan Ram Das Guru

by Amrit Kirtan

(available on iTunes, see resources)

Massage organic sweet almond oil over your face, neck and décolletage.

Step into the bath. Be careful, especially as the salts can make it slippery.

Use a soft wash cloth to gently wash your whole body.

Lie back and absorb all the beautiful vibes. When you get out of the bath, massage your whole body with organic sweet almond oil.

yogi tea

The beautiful aroma of this Yogi Tea will fill your home or studio while it brews.

Based on the knowledge of Ayurveda, this delicious tea will lift your spirit and can provide good hydration and energy throughout the day. It is well worth the effort of making tea this traditional way, and it is very easy once you get into the habit. Try making it for 40 consecutive days and note the benefits you experience.

ingredients:

(organic please)

About 1 1/3 cups of filtered water

3 whole cloves

4 whole green cardamom pods, cracked (use a mortar and pestle)

4 whole black peppercorns

1/2 stick cinnamon

2 slices fresh ginger root or about 5–6 pieces of dried ginger

¼ teaspoon black tea

About 1/3 cup nut milk (there is an easy to make macadamia milk recipe in the Third Eye Chakra section)

method:

Bring water to a boil and add spices.

Cover and simmer for 15–20 minutes, then add black tea.

Let sit for a few minutes.

Strain into tall tea glass and add milk.

Sweeten with coconut nectar sugar.

I am in love with the yoni

I love my yoni.

I love your yoni.

Yoni is the most receptive part of the feminine body.

Yoni is the wisest part of the feminine body.

Yoni receives and contains all the things we are scared to look at.

Yoni contains our darkest secrets.

Yoni contains our brightest light.

Yoni contains our power.

If your light burns your own eyes, the yoni will hold it for you.

But once you are ready beloved… She will reveal

Herself, her magic, her wisdom, her deep intuition,
her ecstasy, her nectar, her endless beauty…
And it is all yours for the taking.

Sofia Sundari *(pictured opposite)*

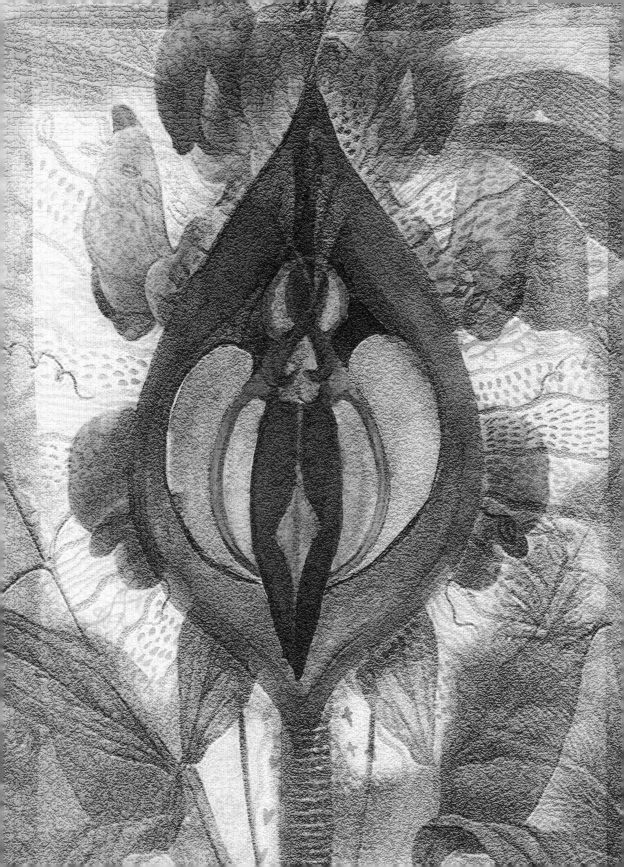

*a journey of self-love
with clarity and power*

manipura, solar plexus

Manipura *(mani = jewel, pura = city)*

Location: *the part of the vertebral column that relates to the navel region*

Associated body part: *abdomen, stomach, upper intestines, liver, gall bladder, kidney, pancreas, adrenal glands, spleen, middle spine*

Related function: *digestion, assimilation, muscles*

Bija mantra: *RAM*

passion Vs anger

This is the centre of personal power, ambition, astral force, desire and emotions based on intellect and touch.

The centre of the third Chakra is located at the navel centre, approximately two inches (5cm) below the belly button. It is the seat of your emotions. This is the energetic centre of empowerment, self-worth, self-esteem and manifestation.

You should move and speak from your navel point – think of it as the centre of an inner star that radiates infinite energy. Confidence is the building block and foundation of the Solar Plexus. This Chakra contains a protective energy against any negativity that may be contained within any of the other Chakras. If one does not have a strong sense of self-worth and understanding of the divinity within, the ability for self-expression will never truly manifest. Your goals may appear to have been reached, but never with a sense of fulfilment and completion if this Chakra is blocked.

This energy centre relates to how we perceive ourselves within society and involves ownership for the choices we make in the face of life's challenges. Young adults between the ages of 15–21 belong in the third Chakra.

This is the time of individual identification, of becoming confident in choices and separating oneself from family constraints and limiting educational systems. In the formative years, we intuitively know that we have a purpose, and if we are given support and freedom, we will naturally be drawn to explore and express it. However, when we are restricted from creative self-expression, we can become resentful, which leads to blind anger. This adolescent anger can block us from accessing the power held in this Chakra and contributes to feelings of powerlessness.

Our work in this Chakra, no matter what our age, is to use the elemental energy we are made of to strengthen our resolve to honour our true Self. Using prana, air and the fire at the navel point, we can access the clearing fire energy that will burn through all blocks and fears. This fire energy, once raised above the diaphragm, can move up into the heart, where the air element ignites true and healthy creative passion.

soul lesson: clarity

When you release all conflict in identity of Self and all images of weakness, you move into an empowered state.

By taking full responsibility for energising your body, keeping it sound and dissolving all cords (subtle energy connections created by the mind) between yourself and others, you are free to be you. Be discerning and ignore peer pressure, be aware that auras and subtle energies are shared, particularly when we are physically close. Competition, power battles, habits and judgements drain your energy and take you away from your truth and your own power. The soul lesson for this Chakra is to go within to generate and harness your infinite energy and use it with clarity. Having an ability to see your truth clearly from source perspective opens the doorway between body and soul and allows powerful energy to flow through your experience. When you choose to live in the 'here and now', guided by an intuitive awareness of your true Self, your visions manifest. When you practise entering the meditative mind, you can know yourself. And when you are listening to the intelligence in your heart and gut, you are not swayed – you stay clearly on your highest path.

Take time to realise the subliminal messages you see in your world and decide which serve you best. Be aware of what you absorb. Be aware of the subtle 'spin' of illusions in all images that you see in media. Self-hypnosis, through meditation with mantra and mudra, will help you stay focused on what serves your 10-body fitness and your dharma. When the hypnotic distraction of the material world pulls you off centre, being in nature can help to bring your third Chakra into balance. Being in sync with the Moon cycles can provide insightful reflections and empower you to manifest your desires. Keeping a journal can assist you in refining and clarifying what you want to manifest. You can also sync your writing up with the cycles of the Moon to further support manifestation. (See resources).

eternal sunshine

I awake ♡

sense: sight

Sight is the sense associated with your third Chakra and the ability to manifest your visions.

Your eyes, ears, tongue, throat and entire nervous system is controlled by the navel point. What do you have in your sights? What do you see that creates desire within you? Are your visions associated with the false ego of the illusionary world, or do they come from the purity and source of your inner wisdom? Our eyes were created ultimately for a broad view of our reality – to see the divine and infinite in everything and enjoy this without attachment. You cannot love, be free or happy if your navel point is not activated and engaged when you look, listen or speak. And although we are not taught to activate the navel point, this skill can be learnt and practised so you can always have presence, balanced observation and enjoyment of life. You can activate your navel centre by pumping it in and out as in the yogic 'Breath of fire'. This replicates the action of laughing, which allows your whole system to relax and enables you to smile and see life with good humour (see resources).

If you do not know how to balance the energy in your third Chakra, you will not perceive the balance of life, the two sides to the polarity in the world. Your navel centre is what intelligently understands balance, and it relays this to your mind. With the power to observe the whole picture, feelings of victimhood, dissatisfaction, resentment and anger dissolve.

An activated third Chakra brings empowered wisdom and courage. Your eyesight can be pulled out of focus if you constantly strain to find joy, answers, knowledge and approval outside of yourself. When reading, focusing on a screen, or looking in only one direction for a long period of time, take breaks and move your attention around, allowing yourself reflection and digestion of information. Shoulder shrugs, side stretches and neck rolls are also great for moving stuck energy caused by holding a concentrated posture for long periods.

element: fire

To truly manifest your desires, digest food and enjoy your life, your power centre should be maintained to 'simmer gently'.

Overambition, excesses and stress can bring this centre to the boil, creating an environment that is too hot and high, potentially leading to 'burn out'. Alternatively, this centre can be too low, through depression, avoidance or neglect, and it can become cold and die down, sinking too low to digest anything. Our lungs are the perfect bellows for this digestive fire – 'Agni' – and with each full, deep breath we take, we fan this fire and bring prana (life force). As we inherit our breathing patterns and nervous system from our birth mother, resetting these patterns to ensure they serve you is a worthy practice. The fastest way to reset your 10 bodies is practising Kundalini yoga, but all authentic yoga and awareness practices that use the breath, sound currents and movement, will work.

The power of what is often called 'God' is behind your navel point. This Light, as pure as fire, gives us strength beyond our muscles and mind. And we can tap into it if we know how. Like a fire, this energy is spontaneous; it happens in the now and when it is fully activated you will know what it is to 'be'. Watch a fire or a candle: it is not stuck; it is so obviously alive in the moment and emits a frequency that appears to dance. You are the same: this energy is within; you are made of this fire. All life happens simultaneously and spontaneously, and you can feel life in this way when your navel point is activated and the fire power of purity is accessed. You are then unstoppable – not thrown off centre by your own or anyone's ego tricks or neuroses. When you know your infinity through a fire that can always be rekindled, you have a tool for experiencing, and therefore realising, your true Self.

Pictured opposite: Palo Santo wood is from the rainforests in Ecuador and is considered by many to be a holy wood. When burned, Palo Santo sticks give off a warm and delicately sweet rose-wood aroma. The Incas have burnt Palo Santo wood since ancient times as a spiritual remedy, for purifying and cleansing.

energy: healer

The happiest people are those who serve others and are always kindly evaluating and improving themselves.

Unhappy people usually negatively evaluate and judge themselves and others. To heal this negativity, bring the clear energy of the solar plexus up to the heart space to facilitate a loving awareness of your true Self. When you sustain loving and empowered self-awareness, you can heal the relationship you have with yourself and all others. Healing the relationship you have with yourself is the foundation from which you can heal other relationships. Ensure that 100 per cent of your energy from your navel point is given to yourself, first, and then you become empowered to serve others. This self-respecting choice comes from a strong third Chakra. You should feel like your true Self – 'light' and not 'heavy' – in all relationships and exude confidence and buoyancy, never feeling as though you should dim the light of your soul. There should also be fluidity and space for honesty, change and peaceful silence.

In your relationships be discerning and ask yourself, 'Can I be happy and free?' 'Do I feel at peace?' 'How is my heart?' 'Can I breathe happily?' 'How is my gut feeling?' To keep relationships healthy, and to heal past relationships, practise yogic mantra and mudra, focusing on activating and clearing the navel point. You can also visualise this centre glowing like a strong yellow sun, dissolving any attachments. Earth's grounding energy and vistas of beauty can help you to remember your true Self and to reflect on what you truly desire. Lie on the earth, with your belly exposed to the sun, and connect with this centre. Imagine a central Sun inside you, energising your whole being. Say to yourself, 'I am free to be me', 'I am empowered to self heal', 'I recognise and tap into the infinite energy inside of me that will never let me down', 'I am who I am and that is that!'

Practise seeing, what you can't see.

So you may find yourself in an experience that you don't like. Perhaps another is behaving in a way that you don't like. You KNOW THAT you CANNOT CHANGE ANOTHER & yet you would like them to behave differently. You KNOW THAT IT DOESN'T SERVE YOU TO SELF SACRIFICE. You KNOW THAT you ARE WORTHY BEYOND MEASURE..... So try this out...... Practice seeing what you can't see, but know you desire. Above anger, frustration, sadness, despair, Above all those emotions is LOVE. Practice seeing this 'other' behaving in a loving way. Hold them in a loving vibe, doing loving things for themselves and others, especially if you can't see it. And enjoy the situation changing.....

...without speaking one word you will effect positive change.

I AM
MASTERFUL

Yes, you have the power in your heart to summon immerse change in your experience. With practice you will become a master of this practice. You will feel empowered and immense joy as you witness situation after situation shift. When you open your heart and feel the energy of non-physical love surrounding you, you draw that vibration into your reality and gift it to all that encounter you. You will attract the best from others, you will breathe in love and breathe it out and into every experience. You are at the leading edge of LOVE......

what's not to love

You are loved where ever you are....
you are loved what ever you are...
Source energy knows you are love...
as you move forward you forgive,
accept and view in love...
your whole self

the gift of strength

In the maturity of this Chakra lies the potential to gain incredible physical strength, more than you think is possible.

This centre empowers you to go beyond self-imposed limitations to become liberated and victorious. An arduous awareness practice is the gateway to reclaiming your human sovereignty and your true strength. This is not about just exercising or 'circusing' the body, it is adhering to a wise practice that moves your body in ways that requires courage, develops stamina and changes the patterns of the mind.

If you want to elevate your energy and gain a higher perspective, you must propel yourself to your higher centres, like a rocket leaving the denser atmosphere of Earth.

Once you can sustain energy in the higher Chakras, life will be easier and far more enjoyable. But you have to get there, first, with your own determined focus. The gravity of your past, epigenetic shifts, karma and habits, must be cleared away or you will only have fleeting elevated consciousness.

Yo-yo-ing back and forth between self-confidence and self-doubt is highly uncomfortable. When you drop the perception that you are 'trying', additionally disengage with any weakness in the mind and do what wise teachers ask of you. If you do this you will have an experience of going beyond what you thought possible. When you do your best to show up and keep up, you will see progress and feel empowered – not for perfection but rather progression and an experience of your true Self.

Kundalini yoga is a practice that requires effort, and for you to move your body in unusual ways to create courage and to change old thought patterns. If practised consistently, it will bring amazing results. Do not accept excuses. Use your own navel power to fly high. Others may elevate and raise your spirits, but only you can access the energy behind the navel point to experience sustained strength.

plant wisdom

Plants are wise witnesses to this world, rooted in the present and always adapting intelligently to their environments.

Plants remind us to let go when it is time, without resistance, and to trust in nature. Being a wise witness yourself and seeing your relationship to everything brings you closer to the healing intelligence of the plant world. Plants reflect the beauty of life and the energy that generates, creates and dissolves. It is self-nourishing and relaxing to allow your eyes to follow beautiful nature. Observing the intricate and clever beauty of plants will bring you closer to seeing your own beauty and grace. Take time to notice colour, texture, detail, pattern, shape, form, light, growth. When you bring plants and flowers into your home and workspace, you bring positively charged energy that serves as a reminder to be grateful and present. As you become more relaxed and gentle, you will attract these energies, and allow your inner and outer beauty to rise.

Flowers are symbols and markers for all celebrations of life.

Just as your energy radiates from your Solar Plexus, flowers radiate from their centres, bursting toward life.

When you lovingly give someone flowers, you can clearly see the joy this gift brings and how the beauty of nature touches their heart and lifts their spirit.

If you feel inclined, don't hesitate wearing flowers in your hair, pinned on to your clothes or in a leis to share.

Scatter flower petals around your altar of self-honouring (if you have one) and the entrance to your home, inviting in vibrant new energy.

Put flowers and their petals in your bath and create a visual immersion into love.

Place fresh flowers in imaginative containers throughout your home and see what magic this invites.

A life spent amongst plants and flowers is likely to be long, healthy and happy.

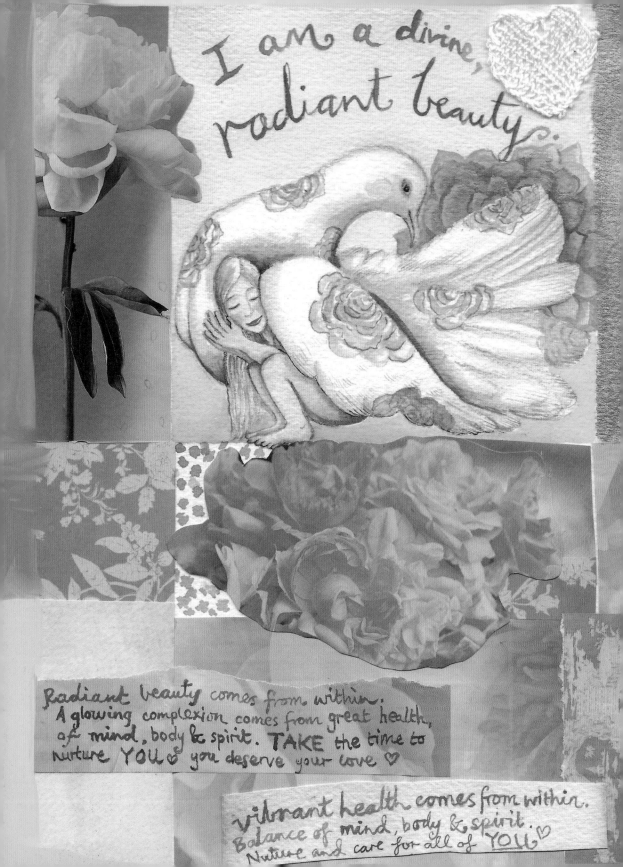

I am a divine, radiant beauty.

Radiant beauty comes from within. A glowing complexion comes from great health, of mind, body & spirit. TAKE the time to nurture YOU ♡ you deserve your love ♡

vibrant health comes from within. Balance of mind, body & spirit. ♡ Nurture and care for all of YOU ♡

sensual therapy

smell

Pure essential oils to work with the Solar Plexus (please use high-quality organic product): grapefruit, petitgrain, fennel, geranium, lemon, ylang-ylang, melissa, black pepper. **Oil applications:** inhalation, bottoms of feet, middle toe, solar plexus

taste

Golden milk is calming for the mind and healing to the body. With all of the added warming spices, golden milk is a great tonic to increase digestion and the circulation. This warming drink also strengthens bones, increases Ojas, cleanses the blood and beautifies the complexion. It's also perfect before bedtime to enhance a sound night's sleep. Google search Ayurvedic golden milk and use nut milk if you are on a plant-based diet.

touch

Crytals to use with the Solar Plexus:

Balancing – Heliodor

Soothing – Citrine

Stimulating – Sulphur Crystal

sound

The mantra 'Har' with the Kundalini yoga meditation for prosperity, practised with determination three minutes per day is very potent.

'This meditation stimulates the mind, the Moon center and Jupiter. When Jupiter and the Moon come together, there is no way in the world you will not create wealth.'

Yogi Bhajan. (See Resources–it is part of the Sobagh Kriya.)

affirmations

I AM CENTRED

I AM DELIBERATELY MANIFESTING

I AM CRYSTAL CLEAR

I AM EMPOWERED

I AM PASSIONATE

I AM FIRST IN MY LIFE

ritual: eating with pleasure

Find beautiful spaces to eat your meals: a room with a view, in nature, or create a favourite nook.

Increase the pleasure of eating by paying attention to the presentation of food and the environment in which you eat. It is very healing to share a meal with a beloved and behold the amazing elemental world. Do you eat by sunlight, sunset, moonrise or candlelight? Do you self-honour and pay attention to your meal? Does it entice you to be still? Where do you buy your food and what is it packed in? How do you store your food at home? Do you lovingly label and arrange your ingredients in a pleasing way? Do you include edible flowers to add colour and beauty to meals? Do you seek the most vibrant local, seasonal foods?

Food is best consumed in the daylight hours, when the fire element is active and eating and digestion is in sync with your body clock. The optimal time to eat the first meal is between 7 and 9am. This meal should contain moisture to help hydrate your body after sleep. It should also contain sufficient energy to support the body through to the early afternoon – the warmest and most active time of day. The mid-meal of the day should be nourishing and joyous – eating to feel satisfied but not too full. The last meal of the day should be the smallest and eaten before sunset or 7pm, depending on which comes first.

This approach to eating supports your physical body, acknowledging the time needed for proper digestion and assimilation of food's energy. Overeating or eating late into the night puts stress on your digestive system and other major organs. Your main organs perform best when you are sound asleep, between 9–10pm and through to 2–3am. This way of eating is a noble practice which recognises that you are a blessed and powerful being who has the gift of free will to create beauty and grace in whatever way you desire.

macadamia, beetroot & cacao celebration cake

This is a moist, delicious cake that is made only with plant food and has no gluten. Perfect for celebrating your Solar Return *(Your birthday is your Solar Return, when the Sun returns to the position it held on your natal chart when you were born).*

Please use only the best-quality ingredients (organic and ethical)

Preheat oven to 180°C

ingredients:

Place the following ingredients, liquids first, into your Vitamix (or similar high-speed blender):

1 1/2 cups water

1/2 cup apple sauce

1/2 cup coconut oil

1/4 to 1 teaspoon pink salt

1 tbsp apple cider vinegar

1 tbsp rice malt syrup or maple syrup

1 tsp vanilla extract

2 medium beetroots (approximately 230g – washed/peeled and chopped)

1 tbsp goji berries (or cranberries)

4 dates (pitted)

1 cup macadamia nuts

1 cup coconut nectar sugar

Beginning on a slow speed and incrementally increasing to high, puree until smooth and well blended. Leave aside.

In a large mixing bowl sift together:

1 cup banana flour

1/2 cup potato starch

1/2 cup tapioca flour

1/2 cup cacao powder

1/2 cup lucuma powder (or carob powder)

1 tbsp mesquite powder (or carob powder)

2 tbsps baking powder (Bob's Red Mill is good, found in wholefood stores).

Spice Mix:

1 tbsp ground cinnamon

1 tsp vanilla powder or essence

1 tsp ground aniseed

1 tsp ground coriander

1 tsp ground liquorice root

1/4 tsp ground cardamom

(If you don't have some spice ingredients, make your own blend to equivalent amount.)

method:

Mix all dry ingredients well. Fold wet ingredients into dry. Pour into a lined baking tin approximately 200mm x 200mm. Bake in the oven for about 35 minutes or until firm to touch and when skewer test comes out clean. Take cake out of tin and place on a cake rack. When cool, dust with a mix of coconut nectar sugar, cacao powder and spices.

Decorate with flowers and enjoy!

crystal clarity

I don't want to use 10 per cent of my brain. I want to challenge myself to use more. I want to explore all the realms of my intelligence: cognitive to emotion, heart math to mystical, common sense to existential philosophy, strategy to divergent thinking. I don't want to sit at a desk, then run on a tread mill. I want to move my physical body to expand and move on par with the flexibility of my mind, my soul. I want to climb, and jump, and stretch, and swim. I don't want to have just a business. I want a cumulative evolution of art, healing, and commerce in the marketplace that not only leverages the impact of my voice and ideas, but everyone who works and collaborates with me. I want to evolve so my ideas evolve, as this world is evolving and requires our best selves. Our quantum selves. I will not be around the doubters, the haters or people who are un-open to the possibility of what humanity can be. We have access to old wisdom, new wisdom, global wisdom. Let's use it. Our becoming is this world's becoming. And I believe there is so much more. Like a child playing this life game, I see constellations of possibility floating a unified field beyond most people's reach. But, I see it. I feel it. And I want to taste it. This is the art of manifestation. Creative evolution is your natural state, always expanding. And when in this current, your being-ness influences the whole world.

When I die and meet my maker, I am going to look back at this life and be proud. I know it. I often sit and talk to my 60-year-old self in meditation. She shows me things. I've sat and talked to my 19-year-old self. I showed her things, how to move, to hold hope. When I was 19, I started having visions of my future 30s self. It brought me to tears. I couldn't believe that was me. Growth, on all levels, thrills me so much that I am so excited about life, and where we will go as a species as we begin to rise up, embodying our encoded genius and changing the direction and narrative on this planet.

Kalisa Augustine (pictured opposite)

you are at the centre
of your world

a journey of self-love
with compassion and joy

anahata, heart chakra

Anahata *(unstruck or unbeaten)*

Location: *heart region of the vertebrae column, centre of the chest.*

Associated body part: *heart and circulatory system,*

lungs, shoulders and arms, ribs/breasts, diaphragm, thymus gland.

Related function: *electromagnetic-field generator,*

blood pressure, immunity.

Bija mantra: *YAM.*

the lushness of
sisterly
love ♡

you
are my sis
eternal
the
live
of life
runs
throu
us,
gonna
it
not
divi

healing
hearts
beyond

I
love
you ♡

understanding Vs judgement

The Heart Chakra is concerned with balancing the love you have for others with the love you have for yourself.

From the ages of 22–28, you are oriented to act from the heart space, coming to understand your life purpose, and hopefully experiencing love and long-standing relationships. If you have been conditioned to judge yourself for being human, you may have felt you had no right to live with purpose. However, living your dharma is your birthright despite discouragement from outdated patriarchal systems (a social system in which males hold primary power). Through an open heart you will understand your humanness and from this centre you will be able to access the vision and wisdom of the upper Chakras. With a heart-centred understanding of yourself, you can become the muse in your life, amused by your own innocence, never ticking yourself off when you fall or stumble. When something goes wrong, you should be able to remind yourself: 'I am not wrong.' Understanding that a liberated heart is a kind and powerful tool will help you release your beloveds with ease and guard your own heart from negative influence.

Judgement based on cause rather than effect is a kinder and more tolerant way to view human behaviours. For example, when another behaves negatively, contemplate the root cause rather than be caught in the effect of the behaviour. With a higher perspective you will discover a greater distance between cause and effect. Rather than be outraged by yourself or another person, you will be empathetic to the life journey and the myriad influences that shape each moment. Become more interested in clearing your own karma and using your heart energy for positive change instead of focusing on and therefore re-creating unwanted events.

When the lotus of the heart opens, you will access consciousness to inform you of the truth of the whole. This sweet understanding will bring tolerance, patience and sacrifice, which will lead to joy, happiness and peace.

soul lesson: joy

If you are to know happiness, you will also know sadness. These emotions come together to create joy.

You must find enjoyment, even with a full awareness of human suffering, otherwise you will suffer too. When you are suffering, you are not able to protect yourself and others or inspire positive change. When you can be curious about the roots of your feelings, the roots that go deep into the mud of life, you will be able to rise from that place as each Chakra's lotus unfurls. You must serve your inner joy by realising it is there in your heart, that it exists without effort and that you just need to be open to receiving the moment without an excuse. With determination, courage, compassion and tenderness, you can allow joy to surface.

Observe how the seeds of your plant relatives survive and then thrive, even after they lay dormant. What does a seed endure? How long does it hold the plan of existence, the blueprint for its potential life? How many months or years does it remain strong, its inner world ready to burst outward, trusting what comes. Go and sit in nature again and again and absorb this wisdom.

Notice the joy that bursts forth without the interference of the human mind.

To practise opening to joy, plant some hardy seeds that will produce flowers. Plant them with love from your heart and tend to them carefully. Watch them grow. Trust the process, nurture them, and allow yourself to feel the joy that comes from the journey. The budding seedling, the plant, the flower, the joy of life expressed.

Joy is to be your journey, a path to remembering your roots and drawing support from the Mother Earth. Water the seeds of your creative Self in the Sacral Chakra and give them infinite power through your Solar Plexus, your eternal sun fire. Now move the prana into the Heart Chakra – where you offer the energy of unconditional love for boundless and limitless growth. Then to the higher Chakras for the sound currents, projection (the vision of our dreams that we project from the Third Eye) and inspired guidance, to fulfil your destiny.

I AM
AN ARTIST

inspired by other artist,
who inspires other artist,
who inspires other artist,
who inspire the creative
essence in other who inspire
the creative essence itself,
who finds joy and peace
and pleasure in creativity!

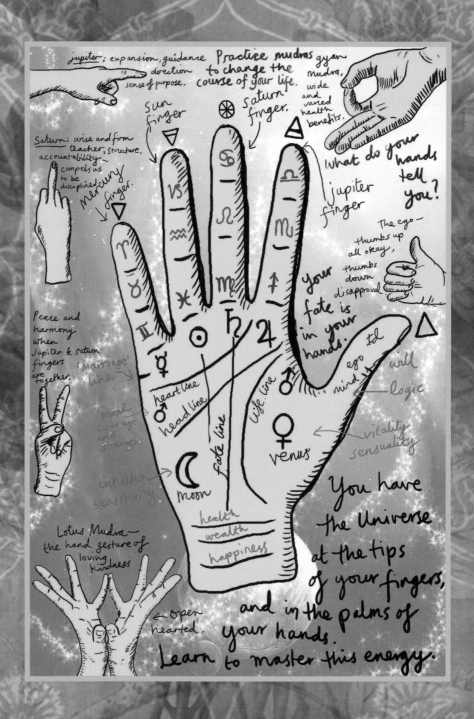

jupiter: expansion, guidance, direction, sense of purpose.

Practice mudras to change the course of your life.

gyan mudra, wide and varied health benefits.

sun finger

saturn finger.

Saturn: wise and firm teacher, structure, accountability — compels us to be disciplined.

mercury finger.

what do your hands tell you?

jupiter finger

The ego — thumbs up all okay, thumbs down disapproval.

Peace and harmony when Jupiter & saturn fingers are together.

Marriage line

moral courage and strength.

heart line

head line

fate line

wife line

your fate is in your hands.

ego mind

Id

will

logic

vitality sensuality

Venus

intuition sensitivity.

Moon

health

wealth

happiness

Lotus Mudra — the hand gesture of loving kindness

open hearted.

You have the Universe at the tips of your fingers, and in the palms of your hands. Learn to master this energy.

sense: touch

Touch is the sense that relates to the Heart Chakra, and this sense offers a profound tool for loving and healing.

This is the energy centre where you hold the image of your divine self, where Earth energy and sky energy touch and unite. Our hands and fingers are a powerful extension of this centre; they are an energy map of our consciousness and health. When you bring the hands together in prayer, you are uniting and balancing both hemispheres of the brain as well as your male and female aspects. Each area of the hand corresponds to a certain area of the body and to different emotions and behaviours. The five elements of the Universe are represented in the five fingers: Thumb (identification) Fire, Index finger (Jupiter finger) Air, Middle finger (Saturn finger) Ether, Ring finger (Sun finger) Earth, Little finger (Mercury finger) Water.

Intentionally curling, crossing, stretching, and touching the fingers and palms in particular ways is known to be using the mudras. Mudras relate directly to the nerves, creating a subtle connection with the instinctual patterns in the brain and influencing the unconscious reflexes in the whole body. Mudras also assist with balancing and redirecting your internal energy, effecting change in the sensory organs, glands, veins and tendons. Using mudras is an essential part of an awareness practice for self-healing. Mudras combined with mantra is a powerful way to rewrite your 'story' and bring you into the present. When you consistently and accurately practise mantra and mudra, you will experience the privilege of self-healing. This is not a miracle; rather, it is a genuine relationship between the physical and the infinite power of the soul's subtle energy. Making healing connections within that brings balance and that creates self-tenderness. If you have ever held a baby's hand in your own, you will have felt the power and the tenderness of life. Your work in this Chakra is to learn how to touch your world with tenderness and loving kindness, and a mastery of the power of the Universe held at the tips of your fingers.

element: air

When you do not consciously breathe you cannot expand; yet breath is life.

The wind opens the heart, the song is released, touching the pearl, the flame and the Moon with infinity.

Prana is life that comes through the element of air, through the breath, and it is given to you because you have earned this life. Because your life, your breath, is a gift, you must receive it and enjoy it fully. This takes practice and a desire to be fully aware. Yogis practise having an awareness of every breath; they understand the immense benefits that come with this moment-by-moment presence. Conscious breathing, called pranayam, gives you prosperity, projection and personality, and increases your aura. Breath of Fire is a practice of continuous breathing, known as one breath. For example, if you practise for an hour, that is one breath. Yogis believe that you are given a certain number of breaths for this life, so for the length of time that you practise Breath of Fire (which is considered a continuous breath) you also expand your life. The longer and fuller your breaths, the longer your life. (See resources).

With an awareness of prana, you can harness the five prana vayus (winds) in the body. These vayus are all of the same energy, just expressed differently. To begin, it's easier to work with an awareness of the first two streams of prana that are controlled by the breath. When you inhale, the first vayus is prana (positive energy) bringing in the life force; the second is apana (negative energy) which occurs with the exhale, and supports elimination from the body. When these two energies meet together at the navel point, they create a pure white heat where lower forms of energy can be elevated. When blockages and impurities in the nerves are removed and the energy channels are cleansed, the kundalini (energy of awareness) can rise and charge up the higher energy centres in the body. Practising breath work, mudras, and applying energy locks (as taught in yogic practices such as the root lock, Mulabandh), these winds can move through you, opening the heart so you may spread your wings and soar high to fulfil your dharma.

energy: healer

The power of the human heart is said to be stronger than 108 Suns.

To clear the Root Chakra you must let go of fear-based attachments. This allows the Sacral Chakra to move through aversions, and the Solar Plexus to see through the lies of the ego. As you work to heal the Heart Chakra, you will benefit from your previous work and learn to simply receive. The joy, the love, the space you want, already exists in this energy centre. As you clear any blind anger in the Solar Plexus, your true power can be seen and harnessed and the red sun of the heart can become warm, tender and healing – fragrant like a rose.

When you feel supported (first Chakra), flowing with creative life force (second Chakra) and work with the infinite energy within you (third Chakra), the lotus in the heart can unfurl, rooted in calm earth, watered with love and fed by the light of truth. An open Heart Chakra is a powerful tool for healing without boundaries and offering the vibration of unconditional Universal love. A truly open-hearted human being is fragrant and alluring. Wherever you go you will magnetically draw out the sweetness of life and goodness in all. When you take responsibility for your energy, showing up consistently for your self-honouring commitments, your inner child can release past hurts and fears, and trust that you are taking the role of the inner parent and living interdependently of others, in your truth. See yourself as whole, as your soul views you – first loving yourself so you can truly love another. Dance in the wild, consciously enveloping your whole Self in your heart's strong, loving energy. Practise feeling completely supported and deserving; allow your cells to spin in joy, dancing into being healed and renewed.

Bless yourself: 'Happiness is my birthright, I wake up to live happiness. I am one. I feel the immense love in every moment. Joy is my experience.'

Ground to Mother Earth, feel the pulse of the Holy Grail that runs through her song lines, feel it rise up through your nadis, into your heart and down through your fingers, reigniting your love for life itself and the sovereign human experience.

SA TA NA MA

By chanting SA TA NA MA we imprint the evolutionary code of the Universe onto our human psyche.

SA is the beginning, infinity, the totality of everything that ever was or will be.

TA is life, existence and creativity that manifests as infinity.

NA is death, change and the transformation of consciousness.

MA is rebirth, regeneration and resurrection which allows us to consciously experience the joy of the infinite. (See Resources.)

the gift of gratitude

Learn to be now.

Place one hand over your heart and the other over your stomach. Breathe deeply and connect these two energy centres. You can do this any time you feel uneasy.

Remember, you chose to be on Earth at this time to experience the rapid evolution of humanity. You were destined to experience vast energetic changes and be a map-maker for the New Earth. Be grateful for your whole journey; appreciate your growth and all the beautiful things you have done.

Practising daily gratitude will open your heart and transform your life into increasingly positive experiences. Keep a gratitude journal and write in it often. When you experience any negative thought patterns, refocus your attention toward love and write down what you are grateful for, in an open stream. What you focus on is what you attract into your life. Hold consistent and gentle appreciation for what you already have and have faith that everything always turns out better than you could imagine. Think of three things you are grateful for. Think of them on waking and each evening before you go to sleep. Then bless every part of yourself; your whole body, the good things you have done for others, your good fortune. Bless every thing; celebrate your life at the beginning and end of every day.

A gratitude practice may take you to the door of awareness. When you embody love you may go through into higher consciousness.

seven principles of huna

Hawaiian Philosophy of Life

IKE — The world is what you think it is (BE AWARE)

KALA — There are no limits, everything is possible (BE FREE)

MAKIA — Energy flows where attention goes (BE FOCUSED)

MANAWA — Now is the moment of power (BE HERE)

ALOHA — To love is to be happy (BE HAPPY)

MANA — All power comes from within (BE CONFIDENT)

PONO — Effectiveness is the measure of truth (BE POSITIVE)

plant wisdom

Plants are the natural food for those who understand that it is a Universal law to have reverence for all life.

Eating a balanced diet of fresh, organic plant foods offers you the life-giving energy you need. It's also a way to easily absorb more prana, to enable the pranic body and the subtle body to join with the soul. Plants carry their subtle bodies with them even when they are picked from their main body, or the Earth. On the other hand, when animals are killed the pranic body is severed from the subtle body without choice. What is left is a decaying body with no life force.

You can find a rainbow of life to eat in the plant world, but green is the colour associated with this central Heart Chakra; it's the healing colour in the centre of the rainbow. Nature offers a wide variety of green plant foods, which help to elevate your energy and assist in clearing out negative and toxic energy from your body. Green foods work to cleanse your liver – an organ that is so vital to your overall health and wellbeing. One of the liver's main functions is to purify your blood on its way through your body to the heart. Someone who has a vital liver is calm, with unerring judgement; they are natural leaders and decision-makers. When the liver is healthy there is a smooth flow of energy through the 10 bodies. There is never stress or tension. When obstructed, stagnant or over-heated, the energy flow in the liver is hampered. This results in myriad physical and emotional problems. Regularly eating appropriate servings of green plant foods, particularly micro algae, salad greens and fresh herbs, will help heal your liver, and in so many ways will lead you to feeling vibrant.

In spring, the abundance of green tips on budding plants is nature's way of calling you to come outdoors and expand and grow. This is the perfect season for cleansing with the help of fresh, young green foods, absorbing all the magic found in chlorophyll.

flower essences

These energetic imprints of the life force of plants work through the medium of water. Plant life force interacts with the subtle bodies of humans and evokes specific qualities within us – in a similar way to inspirational music or art, which carry meaning through sound or light.

the air was fragrant
the earth was soft.
paradise found in truly blessed
gentle gratitude. truly blessed

My own plant Idahs

vibrant
essence magic potions
of life
the
sun kissed collect
the dew flowers this medicine
drenched my love

Use Organic, pure oils & butters to protect & soothe your skin.

Sweet Almond Oil. Apply before showering, once well massage into whole body, take a cold shower, rubbing skin until it feels warm. ☺ The oil will be absorbed deeply this way & you will glow with radiant health.

Use as a sunscreen, protective barrier and a deeply nourishing

Shea Nut Butter.
moisturiser.

10

Protective, sunscreen, repairer

Milk Thistle Oil.

vitamin E Soothing. antioxidant, moisturiser. for face & body.

❋ Keep well hydrated.
❋ Keep out of sun when it is at 90 degrees to Earth, dance in the sun when it is soft. sun rise sun set.

...her beauty touched a part of me that I had not tended loving for eons. Something was waking, stirring, yearning, groaning, begging, aching, calling. I knew it was time to deeply nurture and nourish in a way I was remembering.

A beautiful skin tonic, so reviving ♡ mix equal parts of the extracts of
**Ginkgo Biloba,
Desert Lime,
Kakadu Plum,
& Gotu Kola.**

make your own organic skincare you can find these ingredients from companies that sell 'raw' skincare products.

Apply before adding moisture or oil to face & body. This will nourish your skin with pure plant energy / vibrations of joy & love. ♡♡♡

sensual therapy

smell

Pure essential oils to work with the Heart Chakra (please use high-quality organic product): rose absolute, rose otto, cedarwood, petitgrain, spearmint, eucalyptus, lemon, rosemary. **Oils applications:** inhalation, bottoms of feet, index toe, heart area

taste

Create an elixir for Joy: In a high-speed blender make an all-organic drink from:

1 1/2 cups of filtered water

a small palm-full of macadamia nuts

2 tbsps lucuma

1 tbsp matcha powder

1/4 tsp ground liquorice root

1/4 tsp ground aniseed

1/2 tsp super greens blend

2 pitted dates

few sprigs fresh mint (spearmint is especially lovely for the heart)

ENJOY!

touch

Crystals to use with the Heart Chakra:

Balancing – Turquoise

Soothing – Rose Quartz

Stimulating – Lemurian Seed Crystal

sound

Acknowledging the strength of your heartbeat and enjoying peaceful silence is a powerful way to practise melting into oneness. Sit on your heels with your knees touching your partner's knees. Rest your hands on your knees with palms facing upwards. Fix your eyes on your partner's eyes and concentrate on seeing your own image in your partner. Take long, slow and deep breaths in and out. Create an inner softness by beginning to smile, initiated by moving the tiny muscles in the back of the jaw, towards the inner ears. Project only love and continue sitting in this state for three minutes. To end, inhale, exhale and relax.

affirmations

I AM HEART-CENTRED

I AM LOVABLE AND I AM LOVING

I AM KIND AND I AM FORGIVING

I AM PEACEFUL AND I AM GRATEFUL

I AM PLAYFUL AND I AM JOYFUL

I AM LOVE

ritual:
healing connection

The Earth is a conscious living entity that has begun deep healing.

Energy flows through each of Earth's seven main Chakras and other energy vortices that make up the spiritual body that is our world. Earth's Chakras are connected by energy circuits called Ley or Song lines. This planetary grid system has been known and mapped for millennia. Ancient civilisations revered Earth as a sacred entity and often built their sacred monuments, such as Stonehenge, the Egyptian pyramids, Machu Picchu and other temples, where they considered Earth's highest energy vortexes or Chakras to be. Visiting these sites, especially to meditate and make ceremony, can result in strong connections with Mother Earth, opening your own Chakras, and the ability to be a stronger conduit of divine, creative, Universal energy.

Earth is under stress from growing interference with the flow of Her energy. Deep mining and the alteration of weather patterns undermine Her resources. Widespread interference has resulted in wild weather and an adverse effect on Earth's harmonic balance, her heartbeat and Chakras. As more awareness grows in this Aquarian Age, more communities will come together, using the immense power of united human hearts and creative minds, to restore balance to the whole planet.

When you care for your own Chakra system, and live by your heart, you become part of a solution to heal the planet. If you go deeper into spiritual practice, you will naturally connect with the Earth's sacred sites, Ley or Song lines. She will tell you: 'Together we are stronger than any adversaries.' As we learn more about indigenous communities' ways of living as one with Earth, we will discover a mutual desire to come up with imaginative solutions for sharing resources.

the Earth Chakras

Beloved be free & immortal.

6. 4. ~ Rainbow Serpent

Yin Dragon

7.

5.

Plumed serpent ~ male

find
the Holy
grail.

female ~

2.

3.

Yang Dragon ~

A healthy Earth Chakra has a 777 mile radius (approximately)

1. Root Chakra ~ Mt. Shasta, U.S.A.

2. Sacral Chakra ~ Lake Titicaca, Sth America.

3. Solar Plexus ~ Uluru & Kata Tjuta, Australia.

4. Heart Chakra ~ Glastonbury & Shaftesbury, England.

5. Throat Chakra ~ Great Pyramid, Mt Sinai & Mt of Olives, Middle East.

6. Third Eye ~ this moves ~ currently at 4th Chakra centre in England.

7. Crown Chakra ~ Mt Kailas, Tibet. Himalayas.

Listen to Mother Earth, she has no secrets.

be lush morning smoothie

If citrus or acidic fruit is in season, enjoy some first thing in the morning and allow about 20–30 minutes for digestion. Acidic types of fruit are vibrant and cleansing, a great way to hydrate and receive radiant, clearing energy. Alternatively you could begin your 'breaking of fast' with a large glass of the juice of celery, a smoothie of whole cucumber blended with fresh turmeric or a watermelon smoothie. All the above are wonderful foods that are worth eating for incredible health.

After a rest to digest, follow up with this 'be lush' morning smoothie which is a moist meal and easily assimilated into the body. It also has sufficient calories, protein and carbohydrates to support you in the warmest and most active part of the day — the afternoon.

Method

Place the following ingredients (organic and ethical) in a Vitamix (high-speed blender) and blend until smooth:

2 bananas

2-3 heaped tablespoons chopped papaya

2 dates, pitted

1 chopped apple

Large handful/s of baby spinach leaves or other leafy greens like dandelion or collard.

Handful of berries (preferably wild to your region as these will hold potent adaptogenic energy), fresh, frozen or dried

1 1/2 teaspoons super green blend (preferably with micro algae including spirulina and chlorella, barley and wheat grasses and might also contain raw sprouted green vegetables and raw green leaves and herbs)

1 tsp moringa powder

1 cup filtered water

(Easy to clean, reusable stainless steel straws are great to use.)

brave-hearted beauty

It took almost 33 years to find my true love. I searched far and wide. I looked for this true love in many places. Mostly the hearts of others. I would look at them thinking 'Is it you?' Not paying attention to my own reflection in their eyes, I just kept searching. The search was hard. It left my heart battered. Having to restart, I sat alone. At the bottom of the barrel. The end of a rope. And that's when I noticed her smiling at me. It took a lot of work to look at her and admit I loved her. For it is truly scary to fall in love with one's self. It's an embarrassing process of sorts, an awkward Bambi legs of a moment. I never thought she could be my true love.

I used to not understand her. She annoyed the shit out of me. I would look in the mirror and think her hair was weird. Her legs were big. She talked too much. She was too excited about life. She was too much in general. She wanted too big of things. She loved too much. She cried too much. She was too emotional. Too sexual. Too temperamental. I starved her.

I beat her up mentally and physically. I was ashamed of her. I tried to make her small. So when I found myself alone with her, falling for her, I had a lot of I'm sorrys to tell her. A lot of tears to shed with her. A lot of forgiveness to ask of her.

A lot of acceptance to give her. So to make up for lost time I try to love her as much as possible every day. Listen to her. Feed her well. Let her play and dance. Some days I slip and that's ok. She forgives me. She knows I love her and there is no turning back.

Hope you find your true love too.

Alexandra Roxo (pictured opposite)

the food
diamond,
keep it real,
eat it fresh

there is
no sin,
the lush
garden is
yours

a journey of self-love
through expressing your truth

vishuddha
throat chakra

Vishuddha (*shuddi = to purify*)

Location: *throat, thyroid, trachea, neck vertebra,*

mouth, esophagus, parathyroid, hypothalamus

Associated body part: *base of the neck,*

throat, carotid plexus

Related function: *metabolism and calcium regulation*

Bija mantra: *HAM*

oneness Vs aloneness

The fifth Chakra is the first of the Chakras that takes you toward higher consciousness and into the realm of spirituality.

The Throat Chakra enhances your ability to communicate, be in touch with your inner voice and be able to verbally express your deepest truth. You act from this Chakra from the ages of 29–35, when you should be empowered to proclaim who you are and stand up for your true Self. When you can speak kindly toward yourself and all others, you are acting from the unified perspective of your higher Self. True unity and awareness comes from connecting with your soul's perspective – understanding there is only an illusionary separation between you and everything that is.

Your work here is to ensure that you are always communicating with an open heart and with soul wisdom. When this Chakra is open, you no longer use language that separates you from receiving prosperity or that plays into victimhood. Rather than look for differences, you can acknowledge common ground because you trust in the mutuality with others. As you spiritually mature, you will know that feeling superior or inferior to any other is just a trick of the ego, pulling you away from your heart.

When you connect the Throat Chakra to the navel point, you will remain empowered and be protected and in command of the release and expression of your own energy. You will feel strong enough to make light and friendly connections without any self-compromise.

Using your intuition to guide you when connecting with others, you can discern what is an appropriate level of relay. Patiently listen and allow yourself time to process what you hear. Self enquire: 'Am I feeling expansive or diminished?' 'Should I pause and breathe?'

The tongue is connected to your nervous system and so nervous chatter or difficulty talking may indicate that the sciatic nerve, your life nerve, is tense. Deeply inhale and exhale: 'AAAHHHH' whenever you feel the chest or throat is restricted.

soul lesson: truth

Your 'truth' is always shifting, leading you to realise your true nature and the things that make your heart sing.

It is vital that you know your truth and are able to clearly express it so your creative identity can flow. Vishuddha is where your creative desires and aspirations are birthed via the breath, the power of sound and the spoken word. The Throat Chakra is functional through the lingams: hands, legs and sex organs. This Chakra is the key for the expression of all Chakras; it holds the power to make or break relationships.

The sacred act of making love begins in the fifth and the sixth Chakras. Using words wisely comes with a respect for the power you hold as a creator of your own reality. As you speak your loving truth, you will be asking to receive that which you honestly desire. Denial and dishonesty affect the energy in this Chakra, and so by tapping into the Solar Plexus and Heart Chakra, you have the strength to speak your truth and clear any blocked energy here. Your thyroid gland, responsible for your metabolism, is related to this Chakra. Speaking your truth will bring balance to this gland.

The embodiment of 'woman' and 'man' has experienced thousands of years of repression and so, inherently, this Chakra can be blocked. As you liberate your own truth and emerge as an Aquarian leader of creative self-expression, you free others from the chains of self-deception, to do the same. Every Chakra is expressed through this centre – every lie and every truth. If you feel something intuitively in the sixth Chakra, this Chakra becomes active and your lips will begin to move. If you feel sexual pleasure, you will automatically make sounds. When you remain in the meditative, neutral mind, you have a clear advantage to expressing your truth because, from this calm place, you can know when and how to express your Self for your own prosperity. The more beauty and grace you express, the more that will come back to you.

SOMETIMES

"No thank you." IS the kindest response.

(then gently smile, enough said.)

A BOY NIPPLE
HEE HEE HEE

ICU

sense: hearing

What do you hear? How do you listen?
Can you be the watcher and observer?

Great yogis have repeatedly advised: learn to listen to everybody very patiently, and act only when you must act. Listening and hearing another person is a great skill and it takes practice to master. Most individuals do not want to hear their own truth from another – they feel they already know it and they are already avoiding it. As tempting as it would be to point out what another person seems to be overlooking, it is far better to wonder, What are they bringing to me that is a reflection of who I am? What am I not prepared to hear from my own Self? What patterns of self-deception have I created so I don't hear my own truth?

Areas of the body that need nurturing are often not heard when your 'monkey mind' is running wild. Are your kidneys, heart, liver or stomach telling you something? Are you overheated, overtaxed or tense? When you take a deep breath, do your lungs easily expand? Are your ribs tight and can you roll your neck easily? Listen and tune in to what your body is saying. Are you dehydrated? Are your yin fluids depleted? Can you soften and be kinder toward yourself in any way? Listen to the dialogue you have with yourself. Are you habitually lowering your self-worth? Be honest with yourself.

Make it a habit to hear your intuition and know your truth. The fastest way to open to your intuition is to listen properly. With attentive listening you can be one step ahead of the moment and therefore have a wise advantage. When you can hear and feel the intention behind the moment, you can respond in a way that expands you.

Listening is one of the most important aspects of spiritual fitness. Without this great skill, your whole health is compromised. There is precious inner guidance given to you for every decision required, like a GPS that always takes you to the right place. Your soul is wise and you will be wise if you tune in and listen to it.

element: ether

The power of this Chakra comes from the subtle realms – the sounds of creation that travel through time-space continuum for the manifestation of reality.

Every sound you make creates an aspect of your reality and one of the most potent tools to creating prosperity is practising mantra. Mantra is a continuum of the sound currents of sacred love. When you can immerse yourself fully in these sound currents, your mind becomes calm and your brain patterns improve.

The science of mantra is ancient and was once widely practised in all parts of the world. Reference to mantra is found in the oldest Vedic scriptures, which are claimed to be more than 5000 years old. 'Mantra' means a sacred utterance, a numinous sound, or a syllable, word or group of words that has psychological and spiritual power. The spiritual, energetic value of mantra comes when it is audible, visible, or present in thought. Many mantras are from the ancient Indian language Sanskrit. In Sanskrit, 'man'

means 'mind' and 'tra' means 'to free from', so 'mantra' is literally a tool to free.

The language of Gurmukhi, used in chant and mantras in Kundalini yoga, is another powerful command language. These light languages are energetic sound formulas that carry the essence of all aspects of creation. They are not descriptive, like most spoken languages – they are the actual sound equivalent of manifestation. Hence, 'Ananda', chanted repeatedly, will bring one into a state of bliss because 'Ananda' is the essential sound of bliss. Mantra is said to quieten the habitual fluctuations of our consciousness and then steer it toward its source in the Self, bringing about a state of resonance between the individual and the depths of their being. Inside you is the spirit molecule, and through specific sound currents and mudras, you can access this energetic wisdom (see resources).

energy: teacher

Learn to master your vibration.

As you become a master of your own way of communicating, you will feel the power of all spoken words; you will feel the liberation that loving words bring – spoken, sung, listened to and enjoyed – without resistance. You will become more sensitive to the energy shifts through sound, and what is manifested as a result of those sounds. The Throat Chakra is the teacher and the centre where we can find healthy, authentic self-expression. Once the Throat Chakra is awakened, we begin to allow things to happen as they should. Instead of complaining or doubting, awareness in this centre teaches us to accept the unpleasant aspects of life. Understanding that we magnify what we focus on helps us gain perspective and welcome the flow of life. When we keep listening we receive awareness of opportunities to prosper.

Physical problems in the related areas of the body – trachea, cervical vertebrae, thyroid, parathyroid, neck, shoulders, brain stem, throat and hearing – show up as a sign that there is a blockage in this Chakra. Imbalances in metabolism and calcium levels are also related to this Chakra. Rather than use supplements or pharmaceuticals, practising Kundalini yoga can adjust metabolism very effectively.

Opening the Chakras allows the talents of each to be integrated and realised via our soul. The talent of the Throat Chakra is the teacher. It tells us that serving others is what brings us happiness. We are all born teachers, first to ourselves and then to each other. You will gain much wisdom on your journey of self-love, and through this open Chakra you will know when and how to teach others what you have learnt. Sometimes you will teach by example and other times by word. This is how all the great masters have passed on knowledge. The power of the spoken word, with the right intent, is a beautiful teacher. Develop this talent gently and in a way that resonates practically with your own truth.

SHE is 16 times more complex than HE in every way.

HE is contained in SHE, the female contains the male, the WOMAN holds the man in HER orbit, sets him spinning downwards or spiralling upwards, with the frequency of HER thoughts.

The WOMB-man has to take responsibility for what she births, every thought births a calling to every man to take action.

HE is dependent on HER good grace, but his ego has been allowed to lead HIM, wont let him see this, SHE must go first.

GODDESS, THE ONE WITH THE WOMB OF CREATION. YOU are REAL.

If SHE will not recognise the GOODNESS - GODDESS within herself and respect that, HE becomes angry, dying painfully to access his own GOODNESS. HE thrives upon the natural state of beauty SHE breathes, thinks, speaks and births with an open heart.

If SHE refuses to create and chooses to be destructive, HE must honour HER. Millennia of wars came from a repressed WOMB-MAN, denied the ability to create.

Yet no one can take creativity away from a WOMB-MAN but HER, as she was given the gift of freewill and may always choose HER words and thoughts.

And now the WOMAN must go through the thorny wall and chop the neurosis that grows from the insatiable ego, an ego unable to reflect her divinity No looking glass will help her to see, for SHE is the MOON and she must reflect upon HER world. SHE must slow down and smell the rose of her heart and take command of her neurosis. SHE is called to honestly reflect the truth.

I AM BEAUTIFUL, I AM BLISSFUL, I AM BOUNTIFUL.

I AM THE LIGHT OF MY SOUL. I AM.

Where SHE is centred and gracefully present, she will create this reflection over time.

It is your birthright
and the privilege of being human
to command the neural patterns
and frequency in your brain.
Your Mind will still ask you to
do certain things but you can also
direct your mind in what to do.
You can become a deliberate
creator of your own reality.

the gift of command

This gift of the Throat Chakra is that it allows you to speak and ask for what you want, first to yourself and then all others.

The purpose of life is to command time and space – the time given and the space designated to you, from the get go, for fulfilling your dharma. You just need to show up and keep up, ensuring that your own identity, your personality, your mind, body and spirit are in your command. Having command of your thoughts is the most effective way to face your life, and excel. When you hold positive vibrations, you also attract them. Positive words and sounds are very powerful tools for realising prosperity. As you become a master of your own communications, you will feel the power of all spoken words, including positive affirmations, the seed sounds, mantras and chanting. You will become more sensitive to the way sound shifts energy and what is manifested as a result of those sounds.

To be in command of your own life and realise your nobility, you need to find your own affirmations – words that mean something to you to create the basic rules for your conduct. You mustn't look to others for rules or guidelines for how to think and live your life. You are incomparable, unique, and only you know how to stamp out your own self-deception. Once you have come to an agreement with yourself to define your own nobility, you can command your mind to follow that conduct.

Your affirmation should nudge you along, motivating you to improve and sustain an elevated perspective. Command yourself to follow your heart and the truth of your soul, giving you a container for experiences that will simplify your social interactions. The mind will follow the heart, so always live by the heart and soul and refuse to entertain bad thoughts. Challenging meditation practices requiring focus and endurance work to create the courage you need to be solid, keep up with the rapidly changing world, and live by your own loving command.

plant wisdom

Fruit has the capacity to store pranic energy, and this meditation utilises Mother Nature's gift of fruit.

This meditation works beautifully with passionfruit, but you can use any seasonal fruit. Sit in a comfortable seated position, half-lotus is ideal, but any seated cross-legged position is suitable. Feel free to use cushions and a shawl or blanket if you wish. You will also need a knife, spoon and plate to use at the end of this meditation.

Hold the piece of fruit in cupped hands. Make sure you have good contact with the fruit and also that your fingers are open. You can also do this meditation with a partner, which is even more powerful – especially for any relationship that will benefit from healing love. With a partner, sit in any comfortable position facing each other, making a prayer with your left hands, and hold one another's right hand, resting them across your legs. Listen to a beautiful mantra (see resources). Sit up as straight as you can, take a deep breath in, then exhale and look at the fruit, in appreciation. Close your eyes.

Take a deep breath in. Feel your centre, feel your roots to Earth, connect to each Chakra from the Root to the Crown and imagine energy flowing freely through your body. Focus on your heart and feel it open; feel this energy move outwards down to your hands, and feel the energy flow to the fruit and back to you and through your partner if you have one. Offer your love as a healing prayer for everything that needs healing in your Self and all that is. Breathe very deeply in and out. Continue breathing and pour all your love and blessings into each moment. Continue for a few more minutes then take a deep breath in to finish. Hold this breath and allow a burst of love to rise through you. Immediately cut the fruit open, sharing it if you are meditating with a partner. First enjoy its fragrance, its juice, and then savour the flesh. Close your eyes and allow yourself to connect with the vibrant energy. Bless yourself and everything that is. Sat Nam.

sensual therapy

smell

Pure essential oils to work with the Throat Chakra (please use high-quality organic product): lavender, clary sage, geranium, rosemary, rosalina. **Oil applications:** inhalation, back of neck, big toe, thumb.

taste

Fresh, organic, seasonal fruits and vegetables contain the vibrant flavours and nutrients that your body desires and which are easily assimilated. Certain foods speak your language and you must seek them out. If you feel there is a need to add refined salt or sugar to your food so it 'tastes better', become more present and really connect with the food to discover its real taste. Be willing to try different foods and refine your eating patterns.

touch

Crystals to use with the Throat Chakra:
Balancing – Aquamarine
Soothing – Lapis Lazuli
Stimulating – Blue Apatite

sound

Repeat mantras throughout your day and night to elevate your vibes; sing every day to bless your life and express gratitude. Learn how to engage the neck lock so as to communicate with the empowering command that comes from the root of your tongue. You can do this by sitting with a tall, straight spine and engaging the navel point. Lift the chest upward and gently stretch the back of the neck by pulling the chin toward it. The muscles of the neck and face should stay relaxed through the shift of relative position of the chin and chest. The head stays level and centred. You will notice your spine become even straighter.

affirmations

I AM TRUTH AND I AM EXPRESSION

I AM SILENCE AND I AM SOUND

I AM TEACHER

I AM CREATIVE

I AM STILL

I AM QUIET

ritual:
sound bath

Joy is to be found in sound.

The pure sonic waves that ring from Tibetan Singing Bowls allow you to feel the sound as much as hear it. All parts of your body possess a different resonance. In a healthy body each cell and each organ resonate in harmony with the whole being.

Illness is a manifestation of disharmony, stemming from negative emotions held within the body, which leads to an imbalance in the cells or a given organ. Since all form is energy vibrating at different rates, by altering the rate of vibration you can change the structure of form. Sound from Tibetan Singing Bowls also trains the brain to move into the Theta brainwave frequencies that induce deep meditative and peaceful states, clarity of mind, and acute intuition. The sound vibrations impact your nervous system, engaging your relaxation reflex and inhibiting the stress or pain response. The upper end of the Theta brainwave range heals the body, mind and spirit. At 7–8 Hertz cycles per second, our deeper intelligence,

creativity and Self-healing mechanisms are activated in this state. This 'being in the zone' affects one's internal dialogue and the 'inner critic' is quietened.

Crystal bowls are also used for healing. Although they differ in the type of vibrations that they create, they similarly produce amazing energy for wellbeing, peace and balance. Singing Bowls and crystal bowls are sometimes tuned specifically for healing the seven major Chakras. Each Chakra has specific keys for optimal balancing: Root Chakra – C, Sacral Chakra – D, Solar Plexus Chakra – E, Heart Chakra – F, Throat Chakra – G, Third Eye Chakra – A, Crown Chakra – B.

The gong is a supreme healing instrument and when appropriately played the gong sends listeners into an otherworldly realm, massaging and soothing every cell in their bodies with a pure vibration. Play a gong recording all through the night to invoke a very deep, restful sleep.

sweet bliss balls

dry ingredients:

1/3 cup raw cacao powder

1/3 cup of lucuma powder

1 tbsp mesquite powder

1/4 cup carob powder

(The above ingredients may be substituted e.g you could use carob instead of cacao, mesquite and/or lucuma)

1/4 cup banana flour

1/4 cup coconut nectar sugar

2 tsps ground cinnamon

1/2 tsp ground liqioorice root

1/2 tsp ground aniseed

1/2 tsp ground coriander seeds

1/2 tsp vanilla powder

1/2 cup desiccated coconut

dried fruits:

8 pitted medjool dates

1/4 cup of dried goji berries, cranberries or any other dried fruit of your choice

wet ingredients:

1/2 cup coconut oil

1/2 cup macadamia nuts

1/3 cup of hemp seeds

method:

In a large bowl sift dry ingredients together then mix in desiccated coconut. In a high-speed blender place oil, nuts and seeds Process from low speed to high until the mixture forms a paste. Add the dried fruits and process from low speed to high, pausing when necessary to move the mixture on to the blades, blend until mixture forms a smooth paste. Add to dry ingredients in bowl and mix well, by hand. Refrigerate the mix until firm before making into balls by scooping the mix out with a spoon and rolling to desired size. Roll in desiccated coconut and/or powders like cacao, carob or lucuma. You can also put them on to sticks and dip them into melted chocolate (the chocolate recipe at the end of the Crown Chakra section is perfect for this). Store these Bliss Balls in the refrigerator.

The truth is, the Bliss Balls are good for you and sharing will increase your satisfaction.

holy

'Holy'
is not a word I use often.
When I do,
it is usually for landscapes,
cloudscapes,
generosity,
kindness,
goodness.

All these are holy to me;
when light shines in a dark space,
or beauty overwhelms my eye.
Holy wonder.
Holy wow.
Holy yes.

One day
I will see ALL OF ME
as holy, too.
Even the dark.
Even the harsh.
Even the mercurial moodiness
that sometimes descends.

This body is
my soul's sacred site of pilgrimage.
This heart is
big enough to hold the cosmos.
This love is
infinite.

Holy.
Holy.
Holy.
Yes.

Jai-Jagdeesh *(pictured opposite)*

find
yourself
here.
create
yourself
now

*a journey of self-love
with intuitive vision*

ajna
third eye

Ajna *(Ajna=command post)*

Location: *above and between the eyebrows,
medulla plexus, pineal plexus*

Associated body part: *brain, nervous system, eyes,
ears, nose, pineal gland, pituitary gland*

Related function: *hormonal and psychological regulation*

Bija mantra: *OM*

vision Vs illusion

The sixth Chakra is the seat of emotional intelligence.

This energy centre opens when you are ready to engage with your inherent wisdom. This involves a realisation of non-duality, the union of mind, body and spirit, and your connection with the Universe and all that is. This centre becomes receptive when you no longer believe in the illusion of lack or victimhood and are excited to enter the deep mystery of life. The Third Eye is located in the middle of the forehead between the eyebrows. The 'temples' are on either side of this energy centre of intuitive power.

You are governed by the sixth Chakra from the age of 36 onwards. You begin to open this energy centre whenever you feel ready to grow your awareness and see past the illusions of Maya (material). The sixth Chakra is the centre of psychic power, higher intuition, the spirit, magnetic forces and light. It is about divine thought, balanced intuition and intellect. The invisible becomes visible when you sustain awareness in this centre of higher wisdom. Spiritual fitness is improved when you keep the sixth Chakra open because you are tuned in to inner guidance. When you are open to the source of all creative intelligence, you allow this higher perspective to flow down through your Crown Chakra into your sixth Chakra. As you become more practised you learn to trust the intuitive wisdom that comes through from the meditative, calm mind. In this neutral state you can allow the intellect to show you how to manifest that wisdom. We are in an age where lies and illusions are broadcast constantly. Some are so subtle that, before you are aware, they can pull your energy back down into fear-based thinking. Be watchful.

Your first tool for staying elevated is always the breath. Find a breath-work technique combined with a command that works to keep you open to the present and infinite possibilities and that allows you to face fear with spiritual maturity. As you become more self-aware you will witness and feel the positive power of your true Self.

soul lesson: perception

Who do you think you are? Do you know your value?
Do you know what's real? Do you know your soul?

Children who experience trauma have a tendency to disengage from the lower Chakras and live in the fantasy of the mind. If long-term escapism through imagination and visualisation are practised, it can lead to being a dreamer rather than a doer. If you are unable to make a clear, positively charged decision in nine seconds, your neuroses will fill the gap in your mind. When negatively charged thought patterns are activated, the subconscious mind can take you further into confusion. self-doubt instantly depletes you of at least 30 per cent of your energy.

If you feel washed around by your own indecisiveness, you will probably experience a sense of being a victim in the chaos of your mind. And as you create your experiences by how you think and feel, this will lead you to an unhappy place. When your mind produces endless unconstructive thoughts, it prevents a healthy and fully functional pineal gland, which is vital for intuition. However, when you are grounded in the present moment and are able to open this energy centre, you are self-motivated and know what your next right action should be. Your intuition will lead you to being a seer, serving to perceive opportunities and promptly taking the next right action toward living your non-aggressive, creative life path.

This Chakra purifies negative tendencies and eliminates self-destructive attitudes. When you consciously release old pictures, negative thought patterns and fixed points of view you begin to clear this energy centre. True perception comes from a beautifully clear Third Eye.

Close your eyes and imagine you are sitting opposite yourself, with a lens of higher truth. Can you see beyond self-judgements and criticisms to your miraculous presence? Can you see yourself from 360 degrees and love every aspect? Can you acknowledge your improvements? Can you project the grace of your true Self through this centre?

Look in the mirror and say,
'I love you' If there are tears,
if there is any resistance, listen
to what is behind that and go
deeper into loving that part
   of your beautiful self. ♡

desire to

know

true

self

sense: sixth

The pineal and pituitary glands are associated with this energy centre.

The pineal gland is named so because of its likeness to a pine cone (Latin pinea) and is about the size of a grain of rice. Although science has barely discovered the fullness of its uses in the body or its connection to the mind/soul, the ancient yogis knew it as a vital gland, for many reasons. It is the mind's eye, your sixth sense, and your mind, body and soul's health is dependent on this gland's health. The pineal gland is vital for converting signals from the parasympathetic, to the endocrine, systems. The parasympathetic nervous system incites 'rest and digest, feed and breed' activities via signals such as hunger, satiation, sexual desire, wakefulness or sleepiness. The pineal gland is also responsible for the production of melatonin, from tryptophan. Melatonin helps to regulate the circadian rhythm and plays a role in the timing of puberty. The pineal gland is nourished by the blood – life force, the breath, prana and moving the synovial fluid up and down the spine.

Any 'death' in the blood, or toxicity, easily accumulates in the pineal gland. When it is blocked by toxicity, which includes the accumulation of fluoride, pollutants and negatively charged thought patterns, it is unable to protect you with its ability to bring all-knowing wisdom. As a protective measure from toxicity, this gland will calcify.

A blocked pineal gland is associated with several disorders, including weight gain or obesity, slow thyroid, digestive disorders, kidney trouble, poor circulation, confusion, loss of sense of direction, mood or mental disorders, lack of vision and a lowered IQ. A healthy pineal gland is said to increase your radiance and enhance your overall health, including a healthy nervous-system function, hormonal balance, sleep, focus, cognition, dreaming and imagination.

element: light

The pineal gland resembles the human eye's retina and its function as a light receptor.

Light enters the body through the retinas of the eyes and is sent to the brain, which then sends the light to the gland. Our heart's desires direct our eyes to and from that which we do and don't want. Light activates the gland. In your openness to light information you will begin to trust your intuition and regrade your physical body. You will be increasingly able to fine-tune how you honour your body and fully nurture yourself with clean living. Clean living works to decalcify and reignite the health of your pineal gland, which opens you to the purifying and renewing benefits of light energy. Your life choices should be personally energising and have a positive effect on the health of your mind, body and soul.

Suggested practices for purification of the endocrine system:

• Filter all drinking water to remove fluoride and other chemicals.

• Eat only organic, whole, plant-based foods and only use organic, natural skincare and household cleaning products. Many pesticides contain a cocktail of chemicals that disrupt the major functions that lead to good health.

• Don't consume intoxicants or man-made medications.

• Take time to relax and, with patience, practise presence.

• Ground yourself to Earth and connect to nature every day.

• Allow yourself time to be quiet; just listen. Be asleep by 10pm. Sleep with a gong bath (a meditation played on the gong) or high-frequency sound (currents/music).

• Play high-frequency sound (currents/music) throughout the day, tune out from media that promotes fear or the concept of lack. Be selective in what you tune into; be aware of disruptive, synthetic frequencies.

• Practise authentic yoga every day, which includes meditation with mantra, mudra, and Chakra clearing and aura strengthening.

REFUSE TO DIMINISH
TRUST YOUR 3RD EYE VISION + BECOME
Mentally futuristic
360
degrees
Seer
of all.
intuitive
project
light
vision
wisdom
POWER MULTIPLIED

energy: visionary

Your eyes are associated with this energy centre and they tell much of the soul's journey of unique energy.

Iridology observes the marks and blemishes of the iris, to reveal the wellbeing of the physical body and its organs. Iridology is similar to reflexology, where different parts of the hands and feet are connected to different parts of the physical body and its organs. Marks in the iris can indicate, specifically, where negatively charged energy is held in the physical body. As each organ holds different emotions (for example, grief is held in the lungs), someone holding on to grievance or sadness will have markings in the part of the iris relating to the lungs. Any blockages in the physical body are opportunities to deepen your self-love, clear the past and choose to live in joy.

With an open Third Eye, you can visualise how a change in perspective – perhaps about your past and future – can create miraculous changes. With a consciously inspired perspective, you can project your creative visions so that your life bears the signature of your soul.

As an empowered visionary you will prosper because you will attract what your heart desires. It can then be realised that one doesn't need to look outside of oneself for the sacrament of life, nor should one surrender living an empowered and present journey to another – not to a church, a selectively identified guru, a shaman or any other. The sacred temple inside of you secretes the pleasurable biochemistry of your own human evolution. This temple is yours to sweep clean and enjoy the space of knowingness and deep self-love.

In meditation, using the science of sound, of which you are totally in command, the secretion of the spirit molecule inside of you can be accessed to experience the joy of oneness. You may even experience transcendence if you vibrate the pineal gland appropriately. When you meet the light of your soul in moments of stillness, there are really no words that can fully describe this union. Yet from these experiences you will feel more inner clarity, be inspired to act humbly and touch everyone you meet with the unique song of your soul, in loving and kind ways.

Come down to be here.
Come down from your
fantasy and make reality.
It's safe to be you.
Your body is a safe wonderland.
Come down from the clouds.
Come down and kiss the Earth.
Come down.
Just be you, so we can meet.
Be no one else, I want to
know you.
Just be the light of your soul,
So I can find you♡

e the energy
you want...
to attract

everyone
is
somebody's
weirdo

don't be
normal,
be happy.

the gift of knowing

This gift of this energy centre is an ability to know yourself and unapologetically think, speak and act as your true Self.

The essence of your unique, true Self is love. You should never feel the desire to split your personality so that you fit into somebody else's idea of what being human is. You want to be completely integrated – all your talents merged into one gift of self-realisation that continues to give through a unique, rhythmic intelligence.

Believing that it is appropriate to please others is a conditioned response to childhood trauma. Attempting to please others is very difficult and doesn't serve anyone, least of all YOU. Drop any notion that this behaviour might take you on a magic carpet ride away from conflict; it takes you toward inner, and therefore also outer, conflict.

'Knowing' is not a quest to read people's minds or seek to know what others are up to that needn't concern you. To 'know' is to be mentally futuristic – to be able to watch the weather of life, read the situations you face and act in a way that is self-protective, empowered and kind. As you learn to toggle between different points of view, you become more empathetic toward each individual's experiences. All your relationships benefit when you choose not to argue your perspective, knowing that everyone's perspective is right for them.

Knowing our cosmic history is very important to understanding the cycles of what humanity and Earth is going through, now, and where we might be headed. Your inner wisdom will point you in directions that can bring this knowledge to light. As your perspective starts to widen, victimhood disappears and an interest in imaginative solutions appear. We are at the edge of full disclosure for so many occurrences in our world and Universe, and every human will need to know themselves and what is real. As you develop clarity and calmness, with a strong nervous system, you are better placed to handle the impending expansion in the Age of Aquarius.

plant wisdom

Just as plants need sunshine, so do humans.

Sunlight activates the pineal gland and stimulates decalcifying. Twenty minutes of sunshine every day provides a healthy dose of this radiant energy. Going without sunglasses and a hat is also important so as to receive the sun's rays straight to the brain. Do this consistently and you should notice excellent activity in the gland, when night falls – producing a good measure of melatonin for sound sleep. Avoid sunbathing when the sun is the hottest, around noon to 2pm.

To be well, absorb the sunshine and prana in these foods:

• Each morning, eat citrus fruits or drink the raw juice of lemons. Lemon juice helps to break down calcium deposits and gently cleanses the body.

• Iodine (from dried seaweed) assists the body to release fluoride and is essential for the healthy function of the thyroid gland.

• Boron effectively removes fluoride, helps to build strong bones and muscles, promotes good muscle coordination, healthy testosterone levels and enhanced cognition. This vital mineral is found in plant foods such as raisins, dates, chickpeas, red kidney beans, hazelnuts, walnuts and lentils.

• Medicinal mushrooms, such as shiitake and reishi, oxygenate the blood and cleanse the master glands.

• Other foods that cleanse and nourish the whole body, including the pineal gland, include chlorella, blue-green algae, wheat and barley grasses, basil, coriander, thyme, sage, parsley, turmeric, paprika, cayenne, lavender essential oil, coconut oil.

• Sprouts and leafy greens are majestic foods that when picked and eaten live, straight away from growing organically, nourish you into youthfulness and immunity, strength and vibrancy. Raw, leafy greens, and sprouts in particular, supply protein and bring healthy bacteria into your gut so it can produce vitamin B12.

Door 1

it's pla... your s...

incomparable: Not comparable, admitting of no **comparison** with others, without peer or equal; matchless, peerless, transcendent. No two are the same.

When you hug another for more than twenty seconds, your brain releases endorphins. So enjoy that hug for just a little longer ♡

amour

sensual therapy

smell

Pure essential oils to work with the Third Eye Chakra (please use high-quality organic product): Frankincense, lavender, patchouli, clary sage, cedarwood, rosemary, ylang-ylang, geranium. **Oil applications:** inhalation, under the nose, middle of the forehead.

taste

Why eat organic?

It doesn't cost the Earth; it's a way of eating for the future. Organically grown foods taste better, have more nutrients – vitamins, minerals, enzymes, and micro-nutrients – than chemically grown foods. The soil and land is managed and nourished with sustainable practices via responsible standards. It is the only way to avoid the toxic chemicals present in commercially grown food. Many organic farms grow an assortment of food, taking natural elements and time-tested traditions into account. Diversity is critical to survival.

touch

Crystals to use with the Third Eye Chakra:

Balancing – Labradorite

Soothing – Celestite

Stimulating – Blue Sapphire

sound

Chant the mantra, WAHE GURU.

Wahe is a statement of awe and ecstasy. Guru is the one who brings us from darkness to light. This mantra expresses moving from ignorance to true understanding. It is the Infinite teacher of the soul (see resources).

affirmations

I AM INTUITIVE

I AM PERCEPTIVE

I AM A SEER

I AM VISIONARY

I AM CLEAR

I AM KNOWING

ritual; sadhana

Because you are worthy.

Your predominant life experience should feel vibrant and be a continuum of improvement as you live intuitively and freely, inviting only positively charged energy to be received and to flow through your day-to-day life. The morning practice of Sadhana brings conscious energy and exponential spiritual growth into your whole life. It is a daily prayer that is said by you for you. This practice is not done to please anybody or to gain something, it is what you intuitively know you must do to serve others, live long, and fulfil your dharma.

When you care deeply enough about yourself to take full responsibility for living your life to the fullest, you are ready to commit to this self-enrichment practice. This commitment will create an inner trust and build resilience to disease and disharmony within your 10 bodies. Sadhana is a gratitude practice for your true Self, for your soul's unique vibration and its manifestation in human form.

Sadhana is the main tool to work on to achieve the purpose of life. It can be whatever meditation, prayer and exercise you do consistently. It should work to positively charge you for the day, clearing your Chakras, aura and consciousness, so you can relate to the infinity within you. Before you begin your practice it's ideal to brush your teeth, wash (a cold shower is ideal) and bless yourself.

Sadhana is practised during what are called the 'ambrosial hours' (the two and a half hours just before sunrise), when the sun is at a 60-degree angle to Earth. At this time, the energy you put into your Sadhana will give you maximum results. Also, when the world is quieter, it's easier to meditate and tune in to your own divinity and infinity. When you become skilled at your own self-hypnosis you can stay centred and focused on your life's purpose without being hypnotised by the outer world's drama and illusions. This is not a religious practice; you do not worship anything outside of yourself – rather, it is a practice of self-devotion.

merging

erging

merging

wake up to
your true self

emerging

merging

emerging

answer
the call

merging

I am nourished

macadamia milk

2/3 cup of raw organic macadamias

750 ml of refrigerated cold water

method

Place nuts and water in a high-speed blender. Turn on, moving gradually up to full speed. Blend until just 'milked'.

Turn blender on low for a few minutes to pop a few of the millions of tiny bubbles.

Pour into a glass bottle and keep in the refrigerator.

Before use, shake well.

Keeps for approximately three days.

You can use this milk to make the following drink. Just replace the filtered water with this milk and omit the nuts.

'I am nourished' drink

Place the following (organic) ingredients into a high-speed blender:

1 1/2 cups of filtered water

Approximately 6 raw macadamia nuts (or a palm full – the more macadamias, the creamier)

2 tsps cacao powder

3 tsps carob powder

1 tsp mesquite powder

2 tsp coconut nectar sugar or two medjool dates

1/2 tsp coconut oil

1/2 tsp ground ginger

1/2 tsp ground cinnamon

1/4 tsp vanilla powder or essence

1/4 tsp ground cardamom

1/4 tsp ground aniseed

method

Blend until smooth. This is now ready to enjoy. Add ice cubes if you would like it cold. If you would like to drink this hot, pour into a saucepan and gently heat to desired temperature.

light me up

Last night I dreamt I was pure honey, bathed golden inside and out, made of magikal and medicinal hexagonal honeycomb cells.

Filled with gold.

A living medicine bowl.

Glowing.

Vibrant.

Connected.

Magnificent.

Aligned.

Creator.

A bridge of light.

There was so much ease in my body, supple like a leopard, moving with a deep awareness of my entire being.

Endless mobility, strength, adaptability, trusting I could pivot directions in a seamless nano second.....animal grace.

Power.

Instincts.

Knowledge.

Experience.

I was the Universe.

Stretching golden fingers to reveal new stars, playfully nuzzling mountains. Tickling the chins of great rainforests, the lungs of our mother and sinking into oceans, marrow deep in wisdom and pleasure. My very cells part of the breeze tickling the muzzles of wolf packs running wild. As I ran wild, free, un-tethered. It was absolute perfection, rapture and wonder rolled into every golden droplet.

Truly heaven on the way to heaven is already within me and I am within it.

Gail Love Schock *(pictured opposite)*

*a journey of self-love
through self-realisation*

Sahasrara *(Sahasrara = thousand petal lotus)*

Location: *top of the head, crown, cerebral plexus*

Associated body part: *muscular system, skeletal system, skin*

Related function: *circadian rhythms*

Bija mantra: *OM, AH or silence*

When you are present and attuned to your Sacred heart, you will find heaven to be on Earth. And what you feel to be true becomes your reality♡

reality Vs fantasy

The seventh Chakra is depicted as a thousand-petaled lotus flower at the crown of the head.

This associates with the ultimate awakening and realisation of the illusion of the 'individual Self'. This Chakra awakens when we are finally grounded and open our eyes to see that we have been led to believe that life is meant for 'living'. With maturity it is understood that 'living' is given to you by pranic energy and there is no escaping the reality that you must 'live' through every moment of your life regardless of how it comes to you. If you are sick or struggling, you still must live your life, you must live your life until you pass over. You are here to face the gift of life no matter what arises; this is what it means to be a noble human. When you are in command of your mind, with a strong nervous system, and know how to access the energy at the navel point, you can courageously face every real moment without desire to escape somewhere else.

You become sovereign when you see the world with a sense of wonder, love and unity, while simultaneously perceiving the subtlety of the future as it comes toward you. Reactions are regressions to the past and they surrender your influence on your future. You are, however, regal, crowned by your presence, and you have the capacity to become masterful at this reality and choose how you respond.

When this Chakra is open, you have no desire to escape into any fantasy. Your 'crown' never falls off – you sit and move in a balanced way as grace personified. You know how to have fun and belly laugh, finding humour quickly and dancing with life so that you shake and shape it, not the other way around. When you reach this ultimate, balanced state, you are truly at peace with yourself and the world. You emanate love and wisdom – you are grounded and steady, and materialism and the ego no longer rule you. The polarities of inferiority and superiority are not acted out; rather, the dependable, humble leader rises and patiently listens. The keyword is inspiration, and this energy centre offers a higher glimpse of our role and our destiny. It is here that we learn to trust the inner voice, which we hear when we listen to the wisdom our future Self offers. This Chakra connects to an expanded, Heavenly perspective, where everything in this Earthly reality is viewed as one divine and infinite energy.

soul lesson: presence

Grace all with your presence.

In the here and now, remain open to infinite possibilities. Imagine this Chakra's thousand-petaled lotus of energy opening up and turning downwards, showering your being with the light of your soul.

Through practices that establish a centred state of awareness, the three aspects of being – mind, body and spirit – can come into balance through this Chakra. When the polarities of life can be accepted and integrated, the two wheels of pain and pleasure no longer drive your body/mind vehicle. You take heart-centred responsibility for remaining present, kind and real no matter what arises. If you allow self-love, compassion and acceptance to fill your heart, this energy will flow into radiance at the crown. By letting go of spiritual ambitions and welcoming the joy of being purely present, you become a healer through your noble presence.

When this Chakra is healthy, no judgement is made of any other for where they are on their personal path. As your intuition opens, you become both mentally futuristic and respectful regarding the journey of others. You place your presence into situations that serve you, offering help only when appropriate whilst remaining generous in spirit. The capacity for change increases through generosity. When you let go of desires, knowing that they will be manifested according to your spiritual will, you will become more peacefully present. Your crowning glory in each moment is to realise that it is simply a choice to follow your dharma and that only your mind will stand in your way if you allow it. Know that with the presence a meditative mind brings, the path forward will reveal itself to you. As you move gracefully in spirit toward your true Self, you will find the inner bliss of pure presence, sometimes referred to as Shambala, or Nirvana. When such moments are felt and integrated through your 10 bodies, there is no need for lusting after love or anything else from any other. You are complete; you are in Heaven on Earth.

There was something about her, she had presence, it was as if she was pure and fragrant, beyond words.

magnifique

sense: spirit

Everything exists together as one.

When the energy of awakening rises up through the sushuma (the central passage of the spinal column) to the Crown Chakra at the top of the head, the experience of Samadhi can take place. Samadhi opens us to the highest state of consciousness and inner bliss. It is stepping into your enlightened nature, free from all suffering. Samadhi is found by diving into a consistent state of pure consciousness, void of attachment to any thought. This is a deep, personal, intimate merging with the divine inside and all around you. It is being unified with the Universe through your consciousness. When one reaches Samadhi there is a deep knowing that all is one, and that 'oneness' is at the core of who you are. Samadhi gives you a moment-to-moment spiritual experience that trusts and softens into each new moment of your life. Samadhi is the eternally expanding realisation that your ego is not real, and that you are the infinite soul.

When we open up to greater awareness, we begin to understand that we cannot separate anything – pain from pleasure, the known from the unknown, the past from the future.

It is all one and it all exists together. When we open up to our spirit wisdom, we take responsibility for the infinite power that is within us and inseparable from us. We accept that we must take responsibility for our thoughts, words and actions, ready to work through our life to complete all cycles and let go of repeating patterns. We embrace each season of our life with awareness and preparedness to show up and remain present. In a world where many grown individuals, some who are in positions of great power, act immaturely, like the hurt child or teen, our gentle, calm and wise behaviour provides protection and support to those we are responsible for. Inner and outer conflict dissolve when you step up to your responsibilities and keep up.

Part of the reason religion came to be was because humanity was not ready to accept full responsibility or knowledge. In times of havoc and war, fear can lead to victim consciousness, and a belief that energetic power, 'God', is outside of us. Yet, if you can't see 'God' in one and all, you can't see 'God' at all.

element: cosmic energy

Master your inner energy to create a strong body, so you will have a strong mind. With a strong mind you have a stronger body.

With practice, you can experience infinity (your God Self) within you. This is when you will experience your completeness, your truth, and you will understand that you lack nothing. The chaos of this transitional period on Earth can pull you into a pity pit, or pull you off centre, if you are not aware of your infinity. When you are in touch with your infinity, you are connected to the cosmic energy that is larger than you, that supports you and is 'you'. This connection creates a profound stability in your day-to-day life. When you move your body in certain ways that challenge you to push past the limitations of the mind, you will find an inner strength from the cosmic energy within. It never lets you down and is stronger than your muscles and your mind. You will discover how well you are designed and how beautifully the body heals through a consistent and energetic awareness and self-enquiry practice.

When you access the cosmic energy within you, through the navel point, pure energy bursts up inside, offering inner clarity and strength. This clear energy can be lifted with the kundalini (awareness) coming from the Root Chakra through to the Crown Chakra. When awareness and cosmic energy flow and bring to light your talents held in each Chakra, your Crown opens up to receiving inspiration from your soul. The mind will no longer allow confusion to obstruct happiness. You will consistently circulate and stabilise awareness and cosmic energy up through the higher Chakras. With a clear mind you can make better choices, you are kinder and willing to see things through to the end, patiently manifesting satisfying outcomes. When the illusion of separation from cosmic energy falls away you are able to develop a close relationship with death. This relationship can be used as a tool to help you to be more present, real, and to attend to what matters most to you. You are wise in accepting that the body/mind experience is temporary and it is an opportunity given to embody Universal love.

Muse:
As a verb, to muse is to consider something thoughtfully.
As a noun, it means a spirit, source or person ~
especially a woman ~ who inspires artistic
expression.

we a-muse each other to no end.

I am a muse.

I a-muse myself.

I am beautiful, brilliant, infinitely inspiring,
I am endlessly a-musing!

...taking a visit to savasana......

I am here for
my a-muse-ment.

ਜੇ ਤੁਸੀ ਉਹਨਾਂ ਨੂੰ ਦੇਖ ਸਕਦੇ
ਹੋ ਤਾਂ ਤੁਹਾਡੇ ਵਿਚਾਰ ਕੀ
ਦਖਿਣਗੇ?

What would your thoughts look like if you could see them?

energy: visionary

You won't discover magic through rational thinking, nor will you manifest true prosperity through the emotional body.

If you could see all the times when you became distracted by your subconscious and left a situation just when a door was about to open you would gasp, 'I was sooo close! Wow! And I wanted ... to happen so much and it could have!' Take note of the things that you are focused on and observe how they manifest in your life. What situations do you complain about that keep showing up? If when we don't like something or someone we complain about it, we are giving energy to something we don't want to happen. In this way we can limit ourselves or others. A curse is merely a belief. And it works both ways. If you hold the belief, you are working toward manifesting the belief and magnetising yourself to like experiences.

Mothers hold tremendous power for their children and the vision they see for their futures. A mother's prayer or blessing for her child has the highest energy behind it. However, a mother's worries and concerns also have very powerful energy, as children are easily imprinted with the psyche of their main caregivers. In this Age, as the value of the feminine continues to rise in society, women are increasingly appreciated for all that they do and thereby genuinely encouraged to self-nurture. Millions of women can now connect with each other, find support and create movements for social change that can improve their own health and therefore the health of the community in which they live.

Your work in this Chakra ensures you know your true Self, always see your amazing potential, and are willing to take the responsible action necessary to be fulfilled. To improve everything on Earth, it is important to always envisage all experiences and others in the highest possible light and with the optimal outcome. Sending blessings to everyone and everything will exponentially boomerang blessings back to you. So bless up! You have the opportunity to improve so much in the world around you just with the focus of your thoughts.

connecting with your animal spirit guides

It is no chance that humans encounter specific animals in our day-to-day lives.

The unique set of skills and attributes of each animal on Earth enables it to survive and potentially thrive. Animals carry messages for our spirit. These teachings are also known as animal medicine. This medicine can help us understand our place within the greater world and show us what we may strengthen or dissolve within our personality to refine our vibration. Animal energies influence our lives, just as our energy influences them. Pay attention to which animals show up in your experiences and then enquire about the message that they have for you. It may be the real animal or images or symbols of an animal.

You can tune into animal messages using your intuition. Meditate upon an image of the animal and enquire what message it has for you. Be still and listen for the answer to come to you. For example, the wolf has long been seen as a significant animal spirit guide. The wolf asks you to look within and take command of your life through harmony and self-discipline, to acknowledge that you are wild at heart and yet you appreciate the kind of order that facilitates freedom. A lone wolf evokes freedom; a pack of wolves represents community. Are you a leader? Where could you lead in your life? How could you express your true Self freely whilst still offering your gifts to your community? The howl of a wolf declares boundaries. If you hear this sound or are tempted to howl at the moon, ask yourself, are you clear with others about your personal boundaries? Are your personal boundaries affording you enough freedom? A wolf guides us to our intuitive diplomacy and to being a clear communicator.

I am a fearless
lover of my dream

the gift of connection

Sacred connections to our Universal family are made through an integrated experience of the Crown and Root Chakras.

The feeling of home and wholeness comes with a unity between Heaven and Earth, between mass and ether. Our soul families, our ancestors, the mothers and fathers of our past, are all calling for our healing and for us to remember our human, sacred bind to Earth.

Whales and dolphins have continued with their roles as sea custodians; they hold space for humanity to step up and remember all sacred connections. Surrendering human sovereignty may seem the only solution to survive in the world, but that means giving up being individual in fear of being 'left out' or grasping, striving and pushing for everything needed to live well. However, that is the story that has been created for the benefit of those that chose to claim superiority over others. As these veils of deception lift and we can see layers of manipulation, it is our civic duty to be graceful, grateful and abandon resentment for any part of our journey. We have always been able to choose our attitude and honour our guardian roles. We have enormous opportunities to shift our own habits into loving and healthy ways of living and caring for Earth. Nothing and no one should stand in the way of you connecting to your heart, and self-loving. Go to nature and connect Earth to Heaven and anchor goodwill to this land. Be still and plant your feet firmly on Earth. Feel your auric root bear down from your heels; feel your Root Chakra connect to the planet's crystalline core; open and listen through your heart – you will hear Mother Earth and the voices of your ancestors and spirit guides thanking you and encouraging your self-love to grow.

As we masterfully command our own minds to serve us, we no longer willingly surrender our consciousness. As we choose to consciously create, we will no longer be hypnotised by the outer world. Remembering our gifts and our super powers, we can focus on what we desire and move mountains together with our mastered minds. When connected to all that is, led by our hearts and souls, we are oriented to create a positive future.

plant wisdom

Our heart energy is between Heaven and Earth, between the non-physical and physical realms.

The lower Chakras and the higher centres must remain open to allow energy to flow between these 'worlds'. Anger and pain in the heart disconnects the 'bridge of love and understanding' between Heaven and Earth, which creates fear. If we believe we are helpless, our hearts will bleed energy and feel broken, causing sorrow and despair. When we forget our spirit and live through our emotional body in this way, we can feel angry, lost and confused. The plant kingdom can help to bring you back to reality, to being open, connected and remembering divinity. The soothing green hearts of plants bring calmness to our red hearts. It is a marriage made in Heaven, and our 10 bodies recognise this nourishing and renewing celestial language.

Plant energy calms our nerves – the pituitary responds favourably when we connect with plants. Through the 72 000 nerve endings in our hands and feet, just being barefoot in a garden and 'smelling the roses' can restore inner balance. Plants have a higher state of consciousness and understanding of oneness and no separation – that our wellbeing is theirs.

In a matter of seconds, after inhaling essential plant oil, the plant message, whether it be stimulating or relaxing, reaches the corresponding area of the brain that releases a matching glandular secretion to benefit the body. Plants know what we need; they can read our mind and body, and connect with our spirit. When we approach a plant for food, it intelligently changes its energy to best match what we need, to be well. This intelligence is underlying what makes living plant foods so beneficial.

Intuitively blending herbal teas, picking food and choosing essential oils will connect with your inner teacher, your soul and the souls of plants.

I am
crystal   clear

I am   here
bathed
love &   in
                                light

sensual therapy

smell

Pure essential oils to work with the Crown Chakra (please use high-quality organic product): lavender, frankincense, clary sage, petitgrain, rosalina, vetiver, cedarwood, vanilla, rose otto. **Oil applications:** inhalation, under the nose, top of the head

taste

When you are Raj, you only eat like a king or queen.

You bless your food, you bless yourself, you bless all.

You eat the best quality, freshest, most vibrant plant food.

You eat to balance your 10 bodies and keep your energy flowing and clear.

You take great care in how your food is prepared and presented.

You take time to eat, savouring every bite with due respect to all cosmic energy.

Touch

Crystals to use with the Crown Chakra:

Balancing – Amethyst

Soothing – Lepidolite

Stimulating – Sugilite

sound

To experience the oneness of everything use the mantra 'Ra Ma', in meditation. It works to remove duality, by bringing balance to male and female energies within our psyche. Practice 'Ego eradicator' kriya, prior, as it works to clear the mind (see resources).

affirmations

I AM UNIVERSAL

I AM SPIRIT

I AM SPIRITUAL

I AM CONNECTED

I AM ALL THAT IS

I AM INSPIRING

I AM ENLIGHTENED

I AM ONE

I AM DIVINE

ritual, grounding heaven to earth

Look for rainbows, especially double rainbows, which are becoming more frequent. Take photos of beautiful places in nature and look for orbs and rays of coloured light in the images.

Sit under a tree and daydream.

Just 'BE' in nature. Count butterflies. Listen to bird calls.

Collect the dew from flowers when the first light of day touches them. Drink this dew.

Lie on a carpet of green grass and listen.

Walk in nature, especially alongside a body of water.

Smell flowers and touch their petals incredibly gently so as to leave no mark. Say: 'I love you. Thank you.'

Walk a shoreline in bare feet.

Watch the sunrise and sunset every day for 40 days.

Surf with dolphins.

Whale watch from the shore. Sit on the bottom of the ocean and hear them communicate with each other.

Plant seasonal food, harvesting and preparing it and simply acknowledging gratitude for the rich bounty.

Watch a fire, incense smoke rise, or look into candlelight.

Hug and kiss to greet.

Sit opposite another human being and gaze silently into their eyes.

Make, remake and lovingly repair your own clothes.

Write about things that warm your heart and make you smile.

Take a bath in mineral salts, by candlelight.

Spend time in nature looking at the macro and micro worlds.

Ask a question of a mountain, an ocean, a lake, a river, a tree or any place you are drawn to, and sit still, just listening for the answers that come to you.

Chop wood, carry water.

Breathe deeply more often and sing the song in your heart.

Love your soul.

My happy place is soft and warm and tingly. ∞ I am so into myself. I am so in love with myself, so at peace. I shut my eyes, I breathe in, I breathe out and I float in this syrup of uncondition ∞ of no resistance, I dissolve into me. ∞

cacao yum yum, chocolate

This recipe is GOLD. Make it and you will see what a gift it is that I share with you.

ingredients

(Organic and fair trade, please)

250g raw cacao butter

100g coconut nectar sugar

1/4 tsp finely ground pink salt (like Himalayan)

80g cacao powder

30g carob powder

2 tbsps mesquite powder

3 tbsps lucuma powder

(You can use either cacao or carob powder instead of these two previous ingredients.)

1/2 tsp ground liquorice root or ground star anise, or both

1/2 tsp vanilla powder or 1 tsp vanilla essence

1 tsp ground cinnamon

method

Melt the finely chopped cacao butter, coconut nectar sugar and salt together in a glass bowl, in a 40-50 degree Celsius oven.

Stir about every 15 minutes over the hour or so it takes to melt.

Sift other dry ingredients into melted ingredients and stir well.

hint

At this stage you can add chopped nuts, dried fruit, desiccated coconut, cacao nibs, etc. Experiment – you really can't go wrong because however it turns out it will taste amazing.

Pour into a tray (approximately 20cm x 30cm) lined with baking paper, or into chocolate moulds.

Set in fridge or freezer if in a warm climate or if you want it to set quickly.

Break into pieces and enjoy!

It tastes better when shared, and it makes a beautiful gift.

breathing love

Thousand-petal lotus
Whispering celestial sounds
Received by a body
Well-cared for
I AM the one who dreams awake
Wear me with reverence
With compassion
With humility
Remember
Remember
Remember
S/he who wears a crown
Yet does not
listen
misses the point

When we activate our Crown Chakra, we awaken to the truth of who we are. We awaken to inner wisdom, inner guidance, and experience life as soul embodied. We have compassion for the duality of humanity — including ourselves. From the perspective of our crown, the only time is now and now is always well.

The Crown Chakra out of balance is complacent, out of body, out of touch, escaping. Running away from humanity and fantasizing about somewhere else, somewhere better. Anywhere but here. The Crown Chakra out of balance manipulates and seeks to conquer through psychic abuse.

The Crown Chakra in balance is compassionate. Wise. Practical. Allows us to see from a higher perspective. Breathes deeply. The crown in balance reigns supreme not as a conqueror. The crown in balance reigns supreme in you, in me, as the leader who loves. As the leader who practices, demonstrates, and embodies compassionate wisdom for the highest good of all.

How do we connect to our Crown Chakra?
We tend to our roots.
We nourish ourselves.
We honor the Earth, our body.
We breathe.
We ask.
We listen.
We receive.
One step.
One prayer.
One {deep} breath at a time.

Madeline Giles (pictured opposite)

a journey of self-love
with luminous radiance

aura
8th chakra

Aura (*Aura = the distinctive atmosphere or quality*
generated by a person, thing, or place).
Location: *lies within your physical body, and then*
extends out from your body in an egg shape.
A healthy aura extends up to 9 feet or 2.7 metres.
Related function: *projection, protection.*

light Vs dark

A healthy aura relies upon a strong, healthy mind.

From the state of a strong, calm mind you will become more interested in inner unity and you will understand that your inner peace will be played out in your outer world and can create profound healing. In the neutral mind, you will observe a collective belief that polarities and differences of all kinds should be separated to battle against each other for a winner and a loser. As you become more self-protecting and detach from the outer world's drama, you can choose to strengthen your aura by uniting the male and female energies within you. One more human walking in self-harmony, grounded and projecting calm presence in the here and now, is another step toward collective unity and peace on Earth.

Your eighth Chakra is a living entity, the fingerprint of your soul, the light of your truth and a measurable field of electromagnetic energy that surrounds the body. Everything in existence, even atoms, create an encircling energetic field. Humans are gifted with the ability to strengthen and fine-tune their own magnetic fields using their hearts and minds.

You can work to heal the planet by sending your love and unity consciously through the auric root, into Earth. This stirring of the kundalini energy of awareness in Mother Earth is being performed by many new 'tribes', coming together and meeting at Earth's Chakras. The Rainbow or Yin Serpent is the female aspect of the two great energy lines of Earth; the other, the Plumed or Yang Serpent, is the male aspect. These serpents are made up of male and female currents that intertwine like a Caduceus or 'kundalini' through the landscape. (See the Earth Chakras map in the Heart Chakra section.) The legend goes that when these two serpents encircle the world to meet, and each swallows the other's tail, the resulting united energy is the Earth's 'holy grail'. Our human role is to consciously access this sacred healing energy and relay it back and forth through our auras, increasing its strength and charging its power so it can be harnessed and utilised for the wellbeing of all.

soul lesson: nobility

The eighth Chakra combines the effects, and holds the powers, of all the other energetic centres.

Once you begin to integrate all your Chakras, the aura fully radiates to protect and project you. When the aura is clear of subconscious 'garbage', you attract higher, positively charged energy and are able to intuitively receive guidance from a higher soul perspective. Our aura provides protection against disease and negative environmental influences while also projecting our true nature into the world. A powerful eighth Chakra is noble like gold, automatically deflecting and filtering negative influences, and radiating magnetic vibrancy. When the aura is weak, we behave in a diminished way and are more vulnerable to viruses and the negative and aggressive attitudes of others. If we can extend the aura, the outer arc acts as a filter and a connector to the Universal magnetic field. The outer circumvent field preserves the integrity of the aura. Your aura changes colour and size depending on your mood, your physical health and your spiritual growth. Much can be learnt about your subtle nature through the colour and strength of your aura.

Your opportunity when working with the aura is to ensure that you maintain a noble attitude, even when under extreme pressure. When you behave in a noble manner, you will feel tremendously happy with yourself and satisfied you are making a positive contribution for the betterment of all.

As the patriarchal systems crumble through this Aquarian Age, you can choose to shape the future, by being a noble human. You are here reading this page because you have been stirred to raise awareness into your heart. You are now being nudged to project this powerful energy through your aura and into the world. In your heart you will know if you came here to co-create the New Earth.

Carbon is everywhere – under pressure it is either diamonds or crumbling charcoal.

Be
your
true
self
&
radiate
that
pure
love

once she
decided
to like
herself
everything
changed.

sense: synesthesia

The phenomenon of synesthesia derives from the Greek name meaning 'to perceive together'.

This sensory perception comes in many varieties. Some individuals with this sense hear, smell, taste or feel pain in colour. Others taste shapes, and still others perceive written digits, letters and words in colour. Many synesthetes experience more than one form of the condition. Individuals with different perceptual abilities, who are willing to share their experiences, are leading the way for the world to better understand and respect the power of subtle energy fields.

We have historically been conditioned to think that to be different means to be alone and to perish. However, there are so many people on this planet connecting with others, who have no qualms sharing their differences. It is important to acknowledge how different we truly are and work with these as strengths in relationships, not weaknesses. No two human perceptions can be the same; you cannot truly perceive how another thinks. For example, we have made a collective agreement that the colour blue is a particular type of vibration of light. However, when the vibration of blue is embedded in the spectrum of another colour like green, some individuals have trouble perceiving the subtle difference. If we were all understanding the vibration of blue in the same way, there would be no variation in perception. How you describe blue, what the vibration is to you, and what points of comparison you use will always differ from another person's. True perception for each individual is filtered through the subconscious mind and influenced by personal and cultural symbology. To understand what another perceives and communicates, without misunderstandings, requires stamina, clarity, an ability to listen, and patience.

element: astral light

Astral light is alive and you can imprint the most wonderful ideas into this living library.

This self-luminous, starry light fills the world. This life-force energy holds the memory of everything that was ever dreamt, thought, spoken or created. In this way, astral light is our world's memory and record of the cosmos. All the forms of nature are stored in astral light; everything in the physical world pre-exists in the astral world as an image, type or form, also known as the Akashic records.

Events on this physical plane are also stored; the past is always simultaneously in the now. The pure, trained seer can safely look into astral light and see records past, present and future, all co-existing as a whole. This Aquarian Age is calling for wild solutions to large problems – solutions that may not seem plausible but can be imagined when 'can't' or 'impossible' are dropped. Just as a child might come up with a solution that is imaginative and original, ideas can seem to be just pulled out of 'thin' air with a heartfelt enthusiasm for believing in miraculous

happenings. Allow yourself to daydream on a regular basis – to imagine a different world, society and way of living. Allow yourself to be courageously imaginative and creative. Make mind moodboards and be whimsical. Daydream – giving the brain a rest from thinking. All inspired thoughts go into the astral 'catalogue' of potential realities and they are there for anyone to access through the meditative mind. Your unique perspective is like a shooting star – it will cause someone to gasp and believe that their wishes can come true. The existence of your starry thoughts give momentum to the dreams of others, and so on. This is how worlds are created and transformed.

We have temporarily forgotten that we are the original shape shifters. We must remember how we shape our world and our bodies and always be mindful to choose the highest possible thoughts regarding anything. *Be careful what you wish for.*

energy: guardian

If you could perceive the other 95 per cent of energy that exists around you, self-protection would be more highly valued.

Self-protection is your best tool; you should be your own guardian angel and choose your acquaintances through the filter of a strong aura created by high self-esteem. Think of yourself as a powerhouse of energy that is supporting a small Universe. You host millions of internal and external 'friends' or parasites – from humans to microbes – even ones you have no concept of. Your thoughts, words and actions create your surrounding magnetic field.

Your aura blends with those you come in close physical contact with. In the act of sex, the yin and yang energies merge and the auras blend for what should be a purification. For example, when the act of sex is dysfunctional, lower, non-physical energies are invited to enter the body through subtle energy fields, and then into the Sacral Chakra.

A strong aura is a sacred space of sensitivity that weaves us into the entire Universe and allows us to attract opportunities and wealth. With the aura, we can embody the great human skill of radiance. Within the aura is an Arc line that extends from ear to ear, across the hairline and brow. It's your halo, the nucleus of the aura and the avenue of intuition. This line also relates to the sixth Chakra. Your Akashic records are stored here (the non-physical imprint of all your experience). Women have an additional line between the nipples of their breasts and it is here that an imprint is made of their sexual relationships.

Anything that improves your self-attitude and brings you to a calm, neutral mind, will enhance your aura. Again, back to nature, relaxing and connecting with the conscious energy will assist greatly to clear and strengthen the aura. Daily practices that offer relaxation, peace and quiet should be honoured. Visualise being grounded to Earth, a straight spine, a strong and flexible mind and body. Clearing the Chakras will also ensure the aura is protective.

the gift of dance

To thrive, you must overcome any fear of your own power and foster spiritual resilience and fitness.

Most individuals are unaware of the spiritual warfare that is being used to control the masses. A controlled society that is held in constant fear does not receive the synergetic messages that the Universe wants humanity to download for self-liberation and wellbeing. Being mindful to self-honour means you are able to open to appropriate information and consciously deflect interfering synthetic vibrations that lead to unfounded fears. Creation has provided us with everything that we need to survive and thrive within this Aquarian Age. Your inner power to create positive change is a much-needed resource at this time. Your soul wants you to define yourself at will as your circumstances rapidly change; it wants you to let go of fears and dance with intention directly toward your dharma.

Thunder and lightning in nature create fruitful crops; however, you want to avoid being struck down by the unexpected emotional weather that occurs as the fabric of society changes. A flexible mind and body will serve you very well in these times of transition. Dancing freely and moving the body in unexpected ways, like shaking, helps to break down rigidness in the mind and clears your aura so you can upgrade and integrate new, conscious energy. Dance with the elements; dance on the Earth with bare feet; dance in the rain; dance in the sun; dance at the top of a mountain in mist and clouds and touch Heaven with your heart. Dance all the way through this amazing transition. Dance lightly; don't worry about anything and don't let anyone stop you from dancing with joy. When you are willing to dance forever, you have entered the stream of the soul.

Crystals capture moments of energy dancing with eternity; they hold the beauty of existence in a reflection of miracles of frozen light. Find the right crystals that amplify your personal auric field and inner G (the centred knowing that everything is possible), and wear these to dance with as you reclaim your power on a worldly scale.

plant wisdom

The music of plants is love, and it is heard by the human heart.

The Federation of Damanhur is a group of spiritual communities in Italy that began research into the music of plants in 1976. Researchers at Damanhur created an instrument able to capture the electromagnetic variations of the surface of plant leaves and roots, and turn them into sounds. The results were amazing and it was discovered that trees would learn to 'play' notes with musicians by controlling their electrical emissions as if they are aware of the music they produce. Plants see you as a creative being – works of fine detail that will never be finished. They respond to your imagination and potential. Plants interact and communicate with humans in very subtle ways and the instruments developed at Damanhur offer an opportunity to experience and enjoy this relationship.

You are a relative to plants and when you understand this, you can ask your inner wisdom to guide you to your closest plant relatives.

There are plants that your whole 10 bodies will relay very well with; they will be of benefit, with a love that words cannot explain, a language that is melody heard by your heart and soul.

When you put love out into the world, you cannot imagine how it is going to come back to you, but it will. Our minds are conditioned to want linear, reciprocal and symmetric responses, such as, 'If you do this … that will happen'. Yet the magic of the Universe doesn't work that way. If you choose to connect deeper with the plant world and nature spirits, you will be amazed at the love that comes back to you through the natural world. Unexpected fragrant and beautiful flowers, butterflies, vistas and secluded paths will reveal themselves to you. A wonderland that has existed your whole life can now be perceived. Begin to grow awareness of the magic that plants project through their auras. Value this energy and connect with it. Allow this exchange to become part of your conscious living. Everything is alive in the Universe and has value. Many natural world experiences are priceless and wordless; they offer deeper connections that are beyond temporary wealth or health, and everything to do with true prosperity.

A Woman's eleven moon centres

(Also see resources.)

One. ardine. most sensitive & authentic unmoveable.

The female is a lunar being♡ ruled by the moon.

Two. pinks of the cheeks. watch out ~ prone to misbehave & lack restraint.

Three. lips. private & quiet.

Four. earlobes. up for discussion of values.

Five. back of the neck. Romantic, poetic and perhaps a little Shakespearean foolery.

Six. breasts. overflowing with compassion & generosity

Seven. Navel point. INSECURE!!!

Ten. Clitoris. Social, outwardly focus, eager to meet talk & interact.

Eleven. inner membrane of vagina: into deep, personal sharing.

Nine. eyebrows. dreamy! imaginative goddess visions.

Eight. inner thighs a need to confirm everything.

Each woman has her own individual movement of moon energy through her moon centres. The chin is also a moon centre for men & women. This unique cycle is very subtle and yet also significant as it affects how women experience and relate to everything. Every 2½ days the moon centre changes and this unique sequence repeats every 28 days. By observation and enquiry you can map out your own Moon Centre Sequence. This will reassure you that 1. you are not crazy or changing your mood for no reason 2. You can master your interaction with others by being aware, kind and compassionate towards yourself. 3. You are meant to wax and wane and you cannot control the divine feminine♡

sensual therapy

smell

Pure essential oils to work with the Aura Chakra (please use high-quality organic product): frankincense, lemon myrtle, pink grapefruit, spearmint, vanilla, rose otto, ylang-ylang, melissa, jasmine, neroli. **Oil applications:** inhalation, dilute in water with a disper (an essential-oil emulsifier) and lightly spray all around auric field

taste

Almonds are great for building Ojas. A healthy Ojas helps to create a strong and radiant aura.

Nourishing Almond Ojas Drink

Soak 10 almonds in water overnight.

Blend almonds with a cup of warm water, a pinch each of cardamom, cinnamon and ginger powder, 1 tsp hempseed oil, a few saffron threads (optional) and two pitted medjool dates.

Blend on high until smooth and heat in a saucepan until just warm.

Relax while you drink to ensure your Ojas is restored.

touch

Crystals to use with the aura:

Balancing – Quartz

Soothing – Selenite

Stimulating – White Spirit Quartz

sound

Har Har Har Har Gobinday

This mantra attracts prosperity. When practised with the correct kriya it works magic. Practise it for 40 consecutive days and observe what prosperous opportunities and resources come your way (see resources).

affirmations

I AM NOBLE

I AM LUMINOUS

I AM RADIANT

I AM PURE

I AM VIBRANT

I AM DIVINE

ritual: astrology

The orientation for your experience in this lifetime can be explored and understood by viewing your natal birth chart.

Your birth longitude and latitude reveals much about the areas of human life that you were destined to experience. Your birth mandala is completely unique because it is based on the date, time and place of your birth. Your birth aligns you with your Earth bloodline, a place with a significant connection to the land and potential connections with others, so that you can fulfil your dharma. If you have been led to believe that you were simply to be known by the zodiac sun sign you were born under, you have not viewed your whole Self nor taken advantage of knowing when planets transit your chart.

All wars in modern and ancient times started by using astrology in strategy. Any powerful person understands the play of all Universal influences and uses this information to their advantage. If you are prepared to seek knowledge, you will be amazed in discovering the true order of the world and the depth of knowledge that exists and is used to control those who are unaware. Working with an Aquarian approach to astrology, gathering information about the astrological weather and the planetary transits pertaining to you, you can be prepared for any energetic games ahead.

Every planet and astrological sign plays an influential role throughout your life. Your North Node of the Moon will tell you much about your soul path. Your ascending sign will reveal how you show up in the world – how you are perceived and how you appear to be. The position of the planets relative to each other in your chart will affect many things in your life. Planets can be opposing to one another or complementary and harmonious. If you go in-depth, you will learn much about yourself and you will be able to fine-tune your life and focus on having the experiences you want as well as seeing and resolving soul lessons quickly. You can take your study even further into understanding yogic numerology.

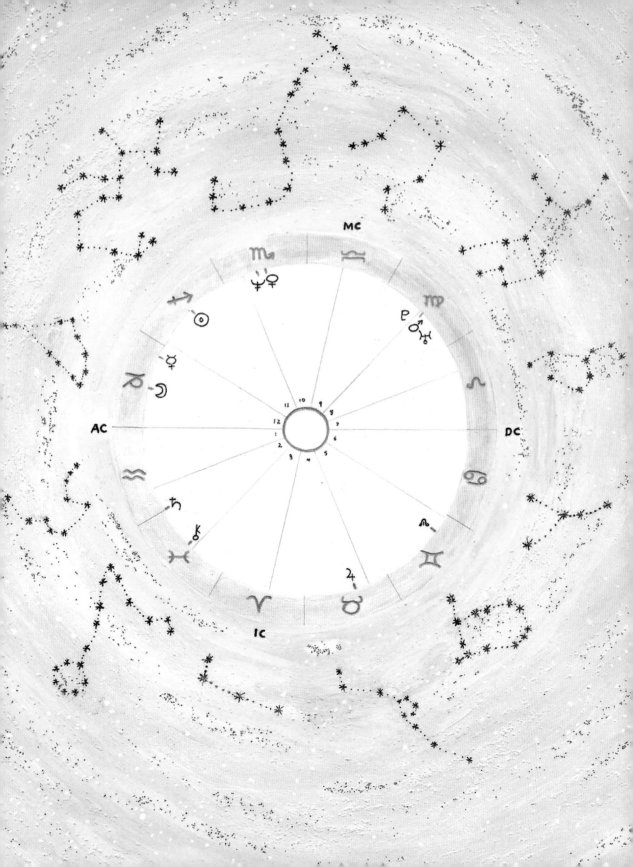

I-am-vibrant raw slice

Radiate with high vibes through all your Chakras and aura with this energising treat. (Please use high-quality organic ingredients.)

base:

1 1/2 cups activated buckwheat

1 1/2 cups shredded coconut

1/3 cup coconut flour

2 tbsp rice malt syrup

Pulp of 2 passionfruits

12 pitted prunes

12 pitted medjool dates

Juice of 1 large orange

Mix buckwheat, coconut and coconut flour in a large bowl. Put all other ingredients into a high-speed blender and puree. Mix with dry ingredients and spread evenly into a 20 cm x 30 cm tray lined with baking paper. Put into the freezer while you make the top.

top:

Place the following into the jug of a high-speed blender:

1 1/2 cup blueberries (preferably grown wild in your region)

4 ripe, medium-sized bananas, peeled

8 pitted medjool dates

Juice of 1 medium lemon plus some of the rind to taste

1 tbsp rosella (Hibiscus) powder. This vibrant superfood is made from the ground calyces of the roselle (Hibiscus sabdariffa) flower, also known as Hibiscus 'Tea'. You can omit this ingredient, however it's a valuable addition to any pantry.

1 tbsp lucuma powder

1 tbsp nopal cactus powder (optional but also a valuable ingredient)

1 tsp ground cinnamon

1 tsp vanilla powder or essence

1/4 tsp ground liquorice root

Blend from low to high until pureed.

Pour into a bowl and stir in 1/2 cup of dried currants (optional), 3/4 cup coconut flour and 1/2 cup shredded coconut.

Smooth over base.

Freeze until firm, and cut into slices. Keeps frozen for around 3-4 weeks.

Serve with fresh blueberries, mint leaves and shredded coconut dusted with rosella powder. Decorate with fresh flowers and bless.

joyful mystic in love

I was afraid of snakes.

When we moved here from a major city, I walked the wild tracks to the beach in fear of encountering a snake. This region is highly populated with snakes, so you will meet them. In the first year, I only saw dead snakes on the road. I became curious and, over time, let go of more than a few of my fears, including going through deep transformation.

The first snake that visited me was a blind snake, it wiggled through our house to meet me in the early hours as I rose for Sadhana. A blind snake is like a very large worm, non venomous and yes, blind.

First message: open up your intuition.

The second snake was a diamond patterned carpet python — a large, elegant creature that came to our yoga studio door as we meditated. I went to the screen door and our eyes met. I was in awe, I was excited and humbled. The incredible flexibility and strength of its spine; it was mystical.

Second message: trust in your powers, have no fear, you can be elegant, quiet, graceful and strong.

The third snake was a bright green tree snake. It waited for me near the entrance to our garden and when I returned home it slithered away, positively camouflaged, merging into the green garden. It raised its head up and with a telescopic vision observed me.

Third message: change your self-perception, look in all directions to find a true perception.

The fourth snake came as I was ready; it was a highly venomous brown snake. My partner found it first and calmly told us of its presence in our garden. It was coiled up basking in the sun. We called the local 'snake man' and he removed it. This was such a profound experience, removing it by force seemed aggressive. The message was clear: the snakes are working the Earth song lines and their work is prevented by buildings, vehicles and many humans.

Fourth message: You are in a direct line with Uluru, the Earth's Solar Plexus. It is important that you help to connect this divine feminine land with this continent's sacred energy centre. Build a spiral out of beach-found rocks and, each day, touch this space and keep the connection open.

The following snake was another carpet python, a beautiful earthy, brown creature, hidden in wild grass. It lay very still as I bent down close and touched the earth nearby. I asked it directly, what message do you have for me? I am learning. I am allowing my heart and soul to lead me into being connected to creatures I had lost connection to. I am remembering. I have done this before and I cannot explain how I know. I also know I am no longer afraid of snakes or any deep transformation. I am in love with all of this very real and mystical journey.

Akal Pritam

Relax

everything always works out better than I can imagine

You are the magician, the master and the mystic in your life.

You can make up any story you want.

You can play with black or white magic.

You can wear a frown or a smile.

And just as you see the reflection of yourself in a mirror, you exist first before the reflection. How you dress and make yourself up happens before your mind sees, and you experience this fully. So with love, be ready to face yourself, see and then let go, ready to improve and elevate yourself beyond self-judgments and ego limitations.

The best advice I can give as you come to the end of this book is to learn to properly relax.

Eat more fruit and relax.

Totally relax.

And then some...

Yes, relax and eat more fruit.

And if there is one other thing I would like you to practise, even before you may come to terms with complete self-love, and that is the affirmation: **'Everything always works out better than I can imagine.'** If you only do one thing each day, use this mantra to steer your mind toward hope, steer yourself away from just believing the delayed reaction coming back to you is as good as it gets. You really do get to choose your own adventure and make it up and change it as you go along. You are allowed to; you are meant to.

The reality that you were born into has so much 'meanness' and repression of human spirit that our perspective of what true relaxation feels like is something we have to remember. We remember this joy when we take our own life into our own loving hands and come home to the being and loving individual that we are, accepting the 'whole' version and overwriting, rebirthing and renewing our living vows. That's what mantras do: they set you in a neutral space and give you a moment to fall in love with yourself, your humanness and your potential, without pressure to be finished, done and dusted. You won't ever be done – you are an infinite soul.

I am what I am and that is that.

Beautiful, Bountiful, Blissful, I am, I am.

Endless blessings to you, love Akal.

resources

Akal Pritam *akalpritam.com*

Working with the Moon:

Astrology Secrets of the Moon:

Discover your true life path and purpose

Patsy Bennett

Moonology: Working with the Magic of Lunar

Cycles Yasmin Boland

Ho'oponopono song

The Mystic Truebudoors, on *iTunes*

Mantra:

Spirit Voyage Mantrapedia:

www.spiritvoyage.com/mantrahome.aspx

Deva Premal and Miten *devapremalmiten.com*

3HO *3ho.org/kundalini-yoga/mantra*

Mantra Artists:

Ajeet Kaur – *ajeetmusic.com*

Alexia Chellun – *alexiachellun.com*

Amrit Kirtan – *iTunes*

Aykanna – *aykanna.com*

BenJahmin-Ji — *soundcloud.com/benjahmin-ji*

Deva Premal and Miten – *devapremalmiten.com*

Gurunam Singh – *gurunamsingh.com*

Jai-Jagdeesh – *jai-jagdeesh.com*

Mirabai Ceiba – *mirabaiceiba.com*

Nirinjan Kaur – *nirinjankaurmusic.com*

Sada Sat Kaur – *yogaborgo.com*

Simrit – *simritkaurmusic.com*

Sirgun Kaur — *sirgunkaur.com*

Snatam Kaur – *snatamkaur.com*

Wah! – *wahmusic.com*

White Sun – *whitesun.com*

Mudra:

3HO *3ho.org/kundalini-yoga/mudra*

Kundalini yoga website –

kundaliniyoga.org/Mudras

Kundalini Yoga Teachers for Kriyas and

Meditations:

Yogi Bhajan – *www.libraryofteachings.com* and

www.yogibhajan.org

Voyage: Search topics under blog –

www.spiritvoyage.com

Anne Novak – *www.annenovakyoga.com/*

GAIA: very large online resource – *www.gaia.com*

Gloria Latham – *www.glorialatham.com*

Gurmukh –

www.goldenbridgeyoga.com/gurmukhs-story/

Guru Jagat, RA MA TV – *www.rama-tv.com*

Guru Singh – *www.gurusingh.com/*

Jai Dev Singh – *www.jaidevsingh.com*

Kia Miller – *www.kiamiller.com*

Kundalini Research Institute –

www.kundaliniresearchinstitute.org

Tommy Rosen – *www.tommyrosen.com*

Search in your home town or city for Kundalini

yoga studios.

Food:

Anthony William. Medical Medium.

www.medicalmedium.com

Earth Chakras:

Earth Chakras Robert Coon –

www.earthchakras.org

With Love and Gratitude for:

Holly Johnson, Darcy Johnson, Aaron Wilson, Julie McCulloch and Kate Hourigan.

My ancestors, my whole family.

My Heart, Soul, Mind and Body.

Mother Earth and all her creatures.

Yogi Bhajan and my yoga teachers.

Carly Loretta, Sofia Sundari, Kalisa Augustine, Alexandra Roxo, Teddy Emerald, Su Graf, Meg Phillips, Asuka Hara, Jai-Jagdeesh, Gail Love Schock, Madeline Giles, Katarina Baliova, Liz Barclay, Alexandra Herstik, Hello Pinecone, Jamal Al-Nabulsi, Mariana Schulze.

Friends of 'The Dispensary'.

The Rockpool Team.

Credits:

Introduction. 'The world is your reflection' and 'Believe in miracles', Talent, Holly Johnson, stargazer.com.au Photo, Meg Phillips.

Root Chakra. 'rooms and womb' Words by Carly, Lorente, Writer, astrologer and wild mama www.herstorycollective.com

Sacral Chakra. 'I love my yoni', Poem by Sofia Sundari, Mystic, tantra and tao teacher, writer. www.sofiasundari.com Photo, Katarina Baliova.

Solar Plexus. 'crystal clarity', Words by Kalisa Augustine, Crystal Bed Therapy, www.kalisaaugustine.com Photo, Liz Barclay.

Heart Chakra. Image opposite 'energy: healer', Talent, Teddy Emerald, Photo, Su Graf. 'brave-hearted beauty', Words by Alexandra Roxo, Transformational coach, healer and writer, www.alexandraroxo.com and www.moonclub.co Photo, Alexandra Herstik.

Throat Chakra. Poem 'holy', copyright © 2017 by Jai-Jagdeesh, www.jaijagdeesh.com Photo, Hello Pinecone Photography, www.hellopinecone.com

Third Eye Chakra. 'light me up', Words by Gail Love Schock, Mind, Body, Soul Medicine, www.gailloveschock.com Photo, Jamal Al-Nabulsi, www.jamaln.com

Crown Chakra 'breathing love', Words by Madeline Giles, Angelic Breath Healing, www.angelicbreathhealing.com Photo, Mariana Schulze.

you are handcrafted
from cosmic
dust,
infinite
nobility♡